Unreal Estate

ANTHONY WOLFF

Unreal Estate

With an introduction
by Stewart L. Udall

Sierra Club   San Francisco • New York

The Sierra Club, founded in 1892 by John Muir, has devoted
itself to the study and protection of the nation's scenic and
ecological resources—mountains, wetlands, woodlands,
wild shores and rivers, deserts and plains. All club publications
are part of the nonprofit effort the club carries on as a
public trust. There are more than 40 chapters coast to coast,
in Canada, Hawaii and Alaska. Participation is invited in
the Club's program to enjoy and preserve wilderness and the
quality of life everywhere. For membership information
and other data on how you can help, please address inquiries to:
Sierra Club, 1050 Mills Tower, San Francisco, California 94104.

Copyright © 1973 by Anthony Wolff.
Part of Chapter 2 appeared in somewhat different form in
New York Magazine under the title, "Invest in the West,"
copyright © 1972 by Anthony Wolff.
Library of Congress catalogue card number 72-89544.
International standard book number ISBN: 87156-074-7.
Type set by Fine Art Typographers, Inc.
Printed in the United States of America

Contents

Introduction

The fast-buck land subdividers of our era are as rapacious and selfish as the timber raiders who cut and burned nearly three-fourths of our nation's forests in the last century. Despite all their pious protestations, their sole interest is in exploiting the land, not in helping people to build homes or create communities. To them, lots are mere chips in a big-money poker game: as soon as the sales contracts are signed, the sharks cash in their winnings and move on to another tract.

The retail sale of lots in remote subdivisions is big business today in every state, and overseas as well. Nationwide, it is estimated that in 1971 625,000 "homesites" were sold by more than 10,000 subdividers for nearly $6 billion. The promoters in this buccaneering business range from "friendly local realtors" to some of the biggest corporations in the country.

In my view, these land speculators have never deserved the recognition they claim as developers. A legitimate land developer makes a massive commitment of time and energy, expertise and capital, to provide the planning, services and facilities essential to a real community, whether it is a complete "new town" or a recreational second-home development. In contrast to the true developer, the subdivision lot seller is a land scalper: with few exceptions, most of the money he invests goes to buy cheap land and misleading advertising, which will enable him to sell quickly at inflated prices. It is surprising to me, as it will be to anyone who reads this book, that the ethical, *bona fide* developers and realtors, whose professions have been besmirched by these land speculators, have not led the fight to curb the excesses of this outlaw segment of their industry.

Indeed, until recently the retail land-sales business has been one of the least regulated industries in the country. Belated efforts on local, state and federal levels to curb the subdividers have only succeeded in curtailing their most flagrant abuses and inspiring them to more insidious methods. Half-truth advertising and high-pressure sales tactics that are no longer tolerated in legitimate businesses today are still the standard tools of the trade for these artful entrepreneurs.

Why, with our awareness of consumer and environmental issues, have we done so little to thwart the depredations of these land sharks? Part of the answer must lie in the fact that land speculation has deep roots in the American psyche. It is part of our folklore that a landlord has a right to make a killing if he can, even at the expense of his unsuspecting tenants, customers, or even innocent neighbors. Land greed has been a prominent trait in the American character from the beginning. And until very recent years, this trait has led us to insist that a landowner has a God-given right to deal with his land as he pleases. Nowhere has the doctrine of *caveat emptor*—let the buyer beware—been applied more appropriately than in real-estate transactions. Gull-them-if-they're-gullible has been the common creed, and the current crop of unscrupulous promoters follows it with a vengeance.

There are some who still argue that the only victims of the subdivision hustlers are credulous customers who should know better anyway. But the fact is that ultimately we are all victimized by these shoddy transactions. The irreparable damage done by the lot sellers has recently been deplored by James Rouse, the justly celebrated developer of Columbia, Maryland, one of the few well-planned new towns that have been built in this country. Rouse describes the cost to be paid by future generations this way:

> Imaginative planning and development of the land is possible today. But not when land has been divided into little pieces unlikely ever to be reassembled. Once the countryside has been given over to uniform quarter-acre or even five-acre lots, you can forget thoughts of clustering, variable den-

sities, common open spaces and the like. Once the acts of registering a subdivision and selling the lots have occurred . . . we have lost the last opportunity for reason and intelligence to accommodate development to the needs of the environment and of people.

Tragically, many areas of our country have already had their options for planned, healthy growth foreclosed by promotional subdivisions. And if our governments on all levels do not take a more active role, much of the best remaining undeveloped land in this country will be so fragmented that sound environmental planning will be impossible in the future.

In this book, Anthony Wolff and the Sierra Club have done some first-rate, responsible muckraking to expose this national scandal, and to identify the flaws in our system that encourage it to persist. Wolff has a keen eye for sharp practice. He has compiled a casebook of outrageous swindles; and he names names, exposes the *modus operandi* of the subdivision hustlers, and traces the aftereffects of their mischief on the nation's citizens and its landscape.

In essence, then, this book is a call for public action. It will take determined and educated efforts by citizens and government institutions alike, all over the country, to stop the subdividers before it is too late. As Anthony Wolff describes it, these modern captains of the Resource Mafia have become very sophisticated at avoiding regulation. If they can get away with their larceny against both the consumer and the land for just a few more years, their wages of sin will be safely in the bank and the damage will be done forever.

Twenty-five years ago, the late Aldo Leopold looked with sorrow on what his countrymen were doing to the American landscape and wrote: "Conservation will continue to get nowhere until we recognize that land is not a commodity, but a community to which we belong." By taking up arms against a gross perversion of the love Americans feel for their landscape, this book seeks to restore that true "community" that can redeem both land and citizen.

Stewart L. Udall
Washington, D.C.
October 1973

Author's note

This book aims to offend only the bandits of the land-subdivision business—those who do mischief to the land and the people. If the book inadvertently slanders legitimate land developers, it is perhaps because they endure their hustling cousins in such close proximity that one can hardly help hitting both with one shot. By way of amends for any unjust injury, however, this book is gratefully dedicated to honest, land-loving subdividers everywhere —whoever they may be.

The research for this book would have been beyond my resources had I not been able to take advantage of the work of others who had been this way before. They are fellow journalists; people in government with long and direct experience with the subdividers; and friends of mine and the land's, many of whom were veterans of subdivision battles long before I enlisted. To all of them belongs much of the credit for this book and none of the blame. Some could not afford to relinquish their anonymity, while others are acknowledged at appropriate points in the text. I could not allow this book to begin, however, without recognizing the special contributions of some.

In California, Lynn Ludlow of the *San Francisco Examiner* generously turned over to me mountains of his files from years of close coverage of the subdividers in that state. Harold Berliner—then the district attorney of Nevada County, now its public defender—offered hospitality and counsel, both of which were rare and stimulating. A former deputy attorney general, L. Neil Gendel, now a public-interest lawyer, guided me through the tortuous legal battles between California and its subdividers. And Elizabeth Fullinwider, at the Sierra Club's San Francisco office, volunteered hours of painstaking research. *Politics of Land* (Grossman), the report of a Ralph Nader study group, was an invaluable reference.

Harvey Mudd and Sally Rodgers of the Central Clearing House in Santa Fe offered a cram course in New Mexico land and water problems, opened their files, and led me to other valuable sources. The thorough reporting of *The New Mexico Review* made my work much easier and the results more interesting than they would otherwise have been.

I also had the advantage of exchanging ideas and materials with Joanna Underwood and Beryl Kuder, both of INFORM, a public-information group specializing in corporate social responsibility. Barbara O. Young typed the manuscript from my runic draft with cheerful forbearance, while Mariana Gosnell copy-edited with welcome intolerance for my misspellings, grammatical lapses and other *bêtises*.

My personal gratitude is also due: to John Mitchell, editor and good friend, for his persistence while I ducked this assignment and his patience while I finished it; to my wife, Pamela, for battling the subdivider in our own backyard while I went looking for trouble elsewhere; to my son, Nicolas, for learning to ride his bicycle without any help from me; and to my daughter, Rebecca, for turning five-and-a-half so gracefully while I was hardly looking.

Anthony Wolff
Truro, Mass.
September 1973

PART ONE

The customer
is
always ripe

1.
The lay
of the land

Truly, wouldn't you like to run away here in this garden of ours? Doesn't your bruised spirit need the soft touch of loving people, your tense body the pure spray of clean, clean air filtered by sunshine? Don't you long for a place . . . where tumbling streams and waterfalls and wave-lapped beaches beg to heal you?

❖　❖　❖

More than ever before, the high profit potential of land investment in the Southwest United States makes this a magnificent opportunity to obtain desirable low-cost property in this high-growth area. Because real estate tends to increase in value during periods of rising prices, your ranch may be considered an excellent safeguard against inflation.

* * *

We're building the planned "new town" of Poinciana, Florida, with thought and care. To keep you in close touch with trees and lakes and lush, green fields. So when you buy property from us for a home or long-term investment, you can get back to nature.

* * *

The most reliable statisticians predict the population of the world will double in the next thirty years. . . . Imagine how the next 30 years of population explosion might force property values to escalate!

In response to such unblushing representations, tens, even hundreds of thousands of Americans are paying some $6 *billion* a year for homesites in far-off land subdivisions with seductive names: Palm Coast, Rio Rancho Estates, Paradise Hills, Sunshine Valley Ranchettes. On the strength of slippery promises and false premises, unsophisticated buyers are sold— for residential use or investment—land that is inappropriate for either purpose. This outrageous deception is the work of bold promoters, including some of the biggest corporations in the country, but their victims are as much deluded by their own naive belief in the American dream of easy money and easy living as they are by the artful subdividers.

There is a long tradition behind today's land hustlers and the land-lust that they both stimulate and exploit. Promoters probably began carving up the earth and selling it off in little pieces the day after Adam and Eve forfeited their unsubdivided interest in Eden and begat the population explosion. It has taken us all of the time since to turn the rest of the world, or most of it, into private property. By the time we got to the New World, the Old one was already subdivided in favor of the rich and the titled. We Americans are, in considerable part, the physical and spiritual descendants of the rest, the dispossessed: landless yeomen, disinherited second sons, daring opportunists, second-chancers—immigrants to whom the lure of free land was perhaps as important as the promise of political or religious freedom.

M. Penn Phillips—a California entrepreneur who is known to his critics as the "Granddaddy of Desert Subdividers" but who prefers the sobriquet "Dean of American Land Developers"—boasts that "the story of America is the story of land hunger and land settlement." At the very outset, in both common men and Founding Fathers, dreams of nationhood danced with visions of the wealth to be made from subdividing an unclaimed continent. "People of all kinds and conditions indulged in land speculation," writes historian Merrill Jensen. "English politicians and bankers and American merchants, planters, small farmers, and clergymen alike took part. It is possible that there were members of Congress who were not speculators, but it is far easier to list those who were than to identify the few who were not."

In the 19th century, land subdivision became the

instrument of Manifest Destiny. Abetted by government policies advancing continental ambitions, land speculators leapfrogged westward, pushing back the frontier. To populate the new land and make the speculator's dreams come true, easterners were enticed to cross the mountains—and Europeans to cross the sea—into the vast American interior. Raucous advertising and elaborate public relations and publicity schemes promised a better life just over the horizon. The effect was not only to dilute the population of the young nation, but also to sustain and amplify the land-madness already inherent in the national character.

Inevitably, the result was an excess of land-selling on one side and land-buying on the other, the direct antecedents of today's scandalous subdivision hustles. The frenzy of land-hungry 19th-century Americans, goaded by free Western land, foreshadowed the blind willingness of Americans in the 1970's to sink their savings in remote subdivision lots.

Historian Daniel Boorstin has described one 19th-century manifestation of the perpetual American land-rush:

> ... on that April day in 1889 when nearly 100,000 men and women—on foot, on horseback, in wagons and with pushcarts— lined up on the border of Indian Territory, waiting for the starting gun to be fired by Army officers. Within a few hours, the 1,920,000 acres of the Oklahoma District had been taken. Few knew why they had picked this plot or that. None knew what

they were missing by not settling here or there.... But they rushed to secure the parcel most to their taste ... or the best parcel left by the faster travelers before them.

The artful deceits standard in today's subdivision promotions are reminiscent of the land-sales frauds of a century ago.

One English observer's description of standard procedure then would serve as well today:

A speculator makes out a plan of a city with its streets, squares, and avenues, quays and wharves, public buildings and monuments. The streets are lotted, the houses numbered, and the squares called after Franklin or Washington. The city itself has some fine name, perhaps Troy or Antioch. This is engraved and forthwith advertised and hung up in as many steamboats and hotels as the speculator's interest may command. All this time the city is a mere vision. Its very site is on the fork of some river in the Far West, 500 miles beyond civilization, probably underwater or surrounded by dense forests and impassable swamps. Emigrants have been repeatedly defrauded out of their money by transactions so extremely gross as hardly to be credited.

But while some things remain unchanged, others do not. Between then and now we have transformed the continent. We have overtaken the receding frontier, and the western horizon hides no new Californias. We are turned back on ourselves and the land we have overrun, to see if we can make some mutual accommodation for survival. In the mid-20th-century context, however, 19th-century land attitudes persist. The distorted land lust of individual Americans is undiminished, along with the land salesman's readiness both to incite and to exploit it. Indeed, with no new land to be pioneered, the public's appetite for even the most unlikely leftover acreage is increased; and increased again by the pollution of air and water and the human spirit in the urban and suburban areas where increasing numbers of Americans feel themselves imprisoned.

It is a bastard business that flourishes on the willingness of people to plunge blindly into land investment on the glib assurances of strangers. It pretends to be part of the legitimate land development industry, which it superficially resembles. But the entrepreneur who carves up remote land for sale sight-unseen on the installment plan is in a different business from the local subdivider who markets suburban lots in the path of urban growth, or the developer who undertakes the creation of a complete "new town" such as Reston, Virginia, or Columbia, Maryland. The entrepreneur is more closely akin to the carnival con-artist, the door-to-door salesman of bibles, pots and pans, home repairs, and the used-car salesman, whose time-tested, hard-sell techniques he has adapted. His business, combining a minimum of land development with a maximum of sleight-of-tongue salesmanship, has no rightful name. For its practitioners, former Secretary of the Interior Stewart Udall aptly suggests the sobriquet "land pimps," with its connotations of the rape of virgin land, and the victimization of a frustrated clientele.

Like any nationwide industry with thousands of independent operators, the promotional subdivision business varies from place to place. Some operations sell desert, others swamps, and still others mountain slopes. Some emphasize the land's supposed recreational and second-home potential, others advertise year-round residential use. Lots may vary in size from quarter-acres to half-acres to two acres, up to five. Investment value is stressed more in some subdivisions than others. There are operations dealing strictly in unimproved land, and purported "planned communities" promising complete facilities. In spite of these local variations, however, the promotional subdivision hustlers can almost invariably be distinguished from legitimate land and community developers by their approach to both the land they sell and the customer to whom they sell it.

The modern land hustler looks for land that has been passed over or abandoned during the past 300-odd years of prodigal, pell-mell development. Often, such land is either too steep, or too wet, or too dry, or simply too far off the path of progress for some reason or other. Perhaps it is range or timberland that willingly supports a modest, honest production year after year, but cannot sustain the rising cost of everything else—or the escalating demands for profit. This kind of land may still be valuable as it is for many reasons having to do with aesthetics and culture and quality of life, but such reasons have no currency in the real-estate market. The land may also be ecologically fragile, as in the case of marshes and swamps, deserts, and high mountain slopes. But by the same token it is usually economically marginal, and that is more important to the subdivider who is looking for raw acreage to buy cheap and sell dear.

Land like this can be found all over the map, despite the promoters' standard warnings that the nation is fast running out of space. The Department of Housing and Urban Development (HUD), which registers these subdividers, lists 2,600 interstate operations selling unimproved lots in every state of the nation except North Dakota. Certain states, however, because of their available acreage, lax land-use and consumer-protection laws — or just because they have a reputation for sunshine, fresh air, natural beauty and similar virtues—are particular favorites of the subdividers. Florida, with its 580 miles of beaches and its waterlogged lowlands, hosted the preview of today's subdivision hustles during the Florida Land Boom—and bust—of the 1920's. For the Florida promoters, the boom is still on: more than 500 subdividers are registered with the state, and they add some 200,000 new acres to their inventory every year. In California between 1960 and 1970, subdividers registered 250,000 acres to be carved up and sold. HUD now lists 561 separate California projects for interstate sale. In the Northeast, where urban pressures are greatest on land and people alike, subdividers in Vermont, New Hampshire and the Pocono Mountains of eastern Pennsylvania offer recreation and refuge from urban pathology. Farther from the centers of population, the vast Southwestern states—Texas, New Mexico, Arizona, Colorado—have become subdividers' playgrounds. Around Albuquerque alone, there are more than enough lots subdivided, or "platted," to double the population of New Mexico, while the state as a whole is overlaid with enough lots—an estimated one million acres of them—to accommodate eight times the present population. Neighboring Arizona has a similar over-supply of subdivided desert acres.

As though there were not enough *Lebensraum* in the United States, the subdividers have gone international. Mail-order subdivisions have been established on obscure out-islands in the Carribean, as well as on Grand Bahama Island itself. From the West Indies, one adventurous developer has hopped to Costa Rica and advertises in *The New York Times* for something called the Beaches of Nosara.

Among the promoters controlling this vast acreage are some certified members of the American business establishment. At the height of its subdivision activities, Boise Cascade—once the 55th largest company in the country on the *Fortune* 500 index—had 17 projects concentrated in California, and a dozen more scattered through the Midwest and the Northeast. ITT Community Development Corporation, a subsidiary of one of the largest corporations in the world, is subdividing almost 100,000 acres of Florida's coastal lowlands. Forbes, the dignified and conservative financial publisher, is selling by mail five-acre "ranches" on its 168,000-acre domain in southern Colorado, "where the deer and the antelope play."

The less imposing names in the business, independents without the resources of large conglomerates, contrive nonetheless to control vast tracts of land. Horizon Corporation has some 155,000 acres—

almost 250 square miles—in a clutch of subdivisions south of Albuquerque, and at least as much in the El Paso area. AMREP (formerly American Real Estate and Petroleum) has almost 100,000 acres northwest of Albuquerque, and other operations in Missouri and Florida. General Development Corporation operates [has] eight subdivisions in Florida, totaling more than 350 square miles, while GAC (formerly General Acceptance Corp.) operates several subdivisions in Florida as well as the 55,000-acre Rio Rico project in Arizona.

Around and in between the major subdivisions, there are others of equal size, and smaller. In some cases, around especially heavily impacted areas such as Tucson and Albuquerque, the subdivisions stand shoulder to shoulder, their billboards lined up along highways in an endless procession of invitations to the good life. Although they are less visible nationally, the smaller subdivisions are so numerous that they represent a far greater acreage total than the larger, more flamboyant operations. The 2,600 subdividers registered with HUD for the interstate sale of a significant number of suburban-size lots provide only a conservative estimate of the number of players in the game. The only subdivisions on the list are those that operate so far from their local marketplace that they solicit out-of-state buyers. Moreover, HUD's Office of Interstate Land Sales Registration complains that there are many delinquents even among those legally required to register.

Together, they hustle a vast domain. There are no precise estimates for the industry, but $6 billion buys a lot of lots. For instance, in New York State alone, in 1971, 91 companies registered with the state to offer 150,000 out-of-state lots for sale to residents of New York, with a total price tag of $375 million. Presumably, some percentage of these lots are bought for reasonable residential purposes. The available evidence makes it clear, however, that the vast majority are bought for speculative investments, or at best with some vague idea of possible future use. Most of the buyers have never seen the land and have neither any idea of what they are buying, nor any good reason to pay so much down and so much a month for ten long years, finally to own a tiny, far-off half-acre of the continent.

In fact, the lots in these subdivisions rarely have any investment value at all, as the testimony of thousands of disappointed owners who have tried to resell has amply demonstrated in one forum after another. Moreover, as places to live, most of these subdivisions have little to offer to justify their prices, which usually include hidden charges that may not become apparent for years. Many promoters are unable or unwilling to supply even basic services to individual lots, much less the complete community facilities implied in their sales presentations. In most cases, the available evidence indicates that the resources of the land itself and of nearby communities are inadequate to support the populations that the promoters blithely project for their subdivisions.

To sell such lots takes considerable ingenuity and a talent for outrageous deception. Local people who know the subdivisions wouldn't dream of buying land there, and they laugh cynically at the city slickers who do. But the people who line up in New

York and San Francisco and Chicago and places in between—and as far afield as Tokyo and Amsterdam —to buy half-acres in the boondocks are arguably sane citizens. They hold down jobs, raise families, even set aside something for a rainy day. Yet, all common-sense evidence to the contrary, they can be deluded into believing that they can find paradise at Paradise Hills, or riches at El Dorado—or for that matter a whole lot of palm trees at Palm Coast or a port at Port La Belle or a city at California City.

If they are so easily deluded, it is perhaps in part because they delude themselves. They cling to the American dream that it is never too late to begin again, or to get rich, if only you have a piece of land to call your own. True democrats, they believe that if the Rockefellers and the Astors and the Carnegies could make money in land speculation—even, more recently, Richard M. Nixon—then there must exist for them the same opportunity. More important to the subdivider promoting an artificial market for his product, the customer is also all too often under the popular delusion that a big company such as ITT or Horizon or GAC, listed on the New York Stock Exchange and all, wouldn't dare sit down with someone, look him right in the eye, and tell a lie. This credulity, carefully nurtured by the companies, all but gives them a license to sweet-talk the customer, to flim-flam and double-talk him.

It is an old-fashioned game, using simple technology. The more ambitious subdividers splurge on indiscriminate mass promotions to flush "live" prospects. Advertisements in newspapers and magazines, or occasionally a full-color Sunday insert, describe the subdivision in extravagant terms—its natural beauty, civilized comforts, climate, booming investment value—and invite reader response. Telephone campaigns are used either to sell lots directly, or to get the prospect to visit the subdivision or invite a sales person into his home. Some of the calls come from distant "boiler rooms," manned by crews of operators with telephone directories and leased long-distance lines. Random mailings invite prospects to cocktail parties, dinners and junkets where they are entertained with elaborate sales pitches. Popular tourist attractions in European cities, or in Tokyo, are covered by "bird dogs," who are paid by the head for delivering culture-shocked Americans to sales meetings. In London, the bird dog might be an attractive English "bird" offering a free bus tour of the city; in Tokyo, the lure might be an invitation to an "authentic" Japanese cocktail party from a kimono-clad Japanese.

Military personnel stationed in Europe get the special attention due a constantly revolving market of 300,000 men—and many of their families—far from home. Men in uniform are recruited to steer their comrades, often of lower rank, to land-sales meetings and dinners. This tactic flouts regulations prohibiting "solicitation involving the general sale of real estate" and soliciting to anyone "who is equal or lower in rank, whether on or off duty, in or out of uniform, on or off a military installation at any time." In an attempt to eliminate such bothersome restrictions on its military sales activities, the Horizon Company and its European brokers hired a consultant named Bruce C. Clarke. General Clarke retired from active duty in 1962 as commander-in-chief of the U.S. Army in Europe. Since then, he has been retained as a consultant to American corporations, including Horizon, "to bring about better relationships between the U.S. Military and civilian businesses." Among his services to Horizon was a promotional mailing sent to U.S. servicemen in Europe entitled "General Bruce C. Clarke, U.S. Army, Retired, Tells Why the Military Man Should Acquire Land." According to *The Stars and Stripes,* authorized publication for the U.S. Armed Forces, Horizon and other U.S. subdivision promoters sell $30 million worth of lots a year to servicemen in Europe.

General Clarke is hardly the only celebrity enlisted in the land-sales business. United States Senator Joseph Montoya as well as Governor Bruce King, both of New Mexico, have appeared in the films AMREP shows at its sales dinners for Rio Rancho Estates. Entertainer Anita Bryant, when not singing the praises of Florida orange juice, promotes General Development's Port Charlotte. Two former Florida governors — Fuller Warren and Haydon Burns—have worked for land-sales companies. The late Chet Huntley brought the residual integrity of a former newscaster to his lobbying and promotional efforts for the Big Sky resort in Montana. Bandleader Skitch Henderson, sportscasters Bill Stern and Red Barber, actor John Forsythe, and the entire Harlem Globetrotters team are among others who have been used in subdivision promotions.

All these efforts—the dinners, the testimonials, the pretty pictures and the rest—are window dressing to attract the real prospects and set them up for the clincher, the sales presentation. From state to state, company to company and year to year, the standard pitch plays the same themes with only slight variations:

- The cities where the prospects live are ugly, dangerous and unhealthy.
- California (New Mexico) (Florida) (Arizona) is beautiful, safe and healthy.
- Population trends threaten an imminent shortage of land in Florida (New Mexico) (Arizona) (California) and promise to drive land values sky high.
- Investment in land is the surest way to financial security and profit for the unsophisticated investor.
- The particular subdivision is ideally situated to benefit from population trends, natural resources (mountains, lakes, seashores) and man-made attractions (Disney World, Cape Kennedy, Las Vegas).
- The subdivision has been professionally planned to enhance the landscape and to provide the services and facilities necessary for a viable community.
- The interests of the subdivider and the prospective customer coincide, obviating the need to seek further advice, and eliminating any risk in buying land from the subdivider.

Such assurances and assertions are supported by statistics presented out of context and without proper qualification, contrived photographs of the land and improvements already in place, and subtly hedged assurances of the subdivider's commitments for the future. Land values are quoted in terms of the subdivider's escalating prices for his lots, to create the impression of rapid appreciation.

The atmosphere of the sales meetings—dinners, at-home visits, subdivision tours—is friendly and casual. But every element is specifically designed to manipulate the customer into signing the contract without taking even the most ordinary precautions, and usually without ever having the document in his own hands until the last moment. Then, if the prospect balks, the sales people have a repertoire of psychological ploys worthy of a CIA interrogator to break down his resistance and lead him to the promised land. The recalcitrant prospect will certainly be flattered; but he (the prospect is usually the husband, with his wife in attendance) may also find his manhood and his concern for his family's welfare questioned.

Doubtless there is something comical in the spectacle of hordes of reckless citizens being gulled out of their common senses by con artists. But $6 billion is a lot of money, and *caveat emptor* is small consolation to someone who has learned the lesson at the expense of his future dreams and his past savings.

Moreover, the customer is not the only victim of the subdivision promoter. Even the minimal "improvements" most subdividers are willing to finance —to make the project look good—do irreparable damage to the land. In Florida, for instance, dredging and canal-building to create salable dry land destroy wetlands, reduce their incalculable economic and ecological value, and threaten the ground-water resource. Earth-moving activities in subdivisions on the steep slopes of California and Vermont invite severe erosion, siltation of waterways, and flooding. Bladed dirt roads in Southwestern desert projects feed dust to the wind. In Minnesota, the sewage from waterfront developments pollutes Lake Superior. To the extent that these subdivisions are actually developed in the future, such problems will become increasingly severe, and the land will suffer the additional impacts associated with large, concentrated populations.

Although it seems far more likely that most of these subdivisions will never be fully developed, they will continue to bedevil the larger political jurisdictions in which they operate. A large subdivision, even a premature ghost town, preempts alternative land uses forever, and frustrates planning for appropriate development, public or private. At the same time, even the slightest population growth in a subdivision can exceed the capacity of the adjacent town or surrounding county to provide essential services.

In the wreckage that promotional subdivisions create are the victims that provide the focus for the following chapters. First are the consumers, who buy the land at inflated prices and pay for it endlessly. Second is the land itself. The third victim is hope for the future—for adequate recreational parks and preserves, for real economic development, for healthy new communities—precluded by the headlong profiteering of the subdividers. The book concludes with a look at what has and has not been done to control the blight.

2.
Guess who's coming to dinner

In this shady corner of the real-estate business, land is not so much bought as sold. By the time he is six, any American child knows not to buy anything sight unseen, lest his sandbox playmates bilk him of his allowance. Soon after, he learns not to put his signature on the dotted line of a contract without going over the fine print with a magnifying glass and a lawyer. To make the prospect abandon the prudent cynicism he learned in the nursery, the promoter must induce in him the same "willing suspension of disbelief" that overcomes audiences enthralled by a theatrical performance.

The customer's encounter with the lot salesman nas indeed been as carefully written, rehearsed and staged as a Broadway play. There is an appropriate bit in the salesman's repertoire for every occasion, but the *piece de resistance*, the one that calls for every trick in his book, is the land-sales dinner. It is an unlikely event: strangers are invited at random to a free dinner, and two hours later they are sold land that they have never seen and know nothing about. Unlikely—but it happens all the time. The technique is used extensively in large urban and suburban communities by such major subdividers as AMREP, General Development and ITT. According to one AMREP's executive, his company fields 17 dinner-sales teams in the New York area alone, and it is not unusual to schedule seven simultaneous dinners on any given evening, feeding and hustling upwards of 1,500 prospects per week. In New York, a free-loader can eat out every night almost indefinitely.

At one New York seance in the spring of 1972, a heavily made-up and ornamented lady named Charlotte was hustling a customer in the dimness of a private room at the Playboy Club. ". . . You get to know me, you see that whatever I can do to help you, I'm there to help you," she was saying. A couple of Bunnies, obviously unhappy with their assignment, served small, watery drinks and second-rate steaks. "So if God forbid there is a problem, you don't have to worry . . . Any problem that you have, I take care of it for you."

What Charlotte is hustling with such ardor is not her considerable charms, but a half-acre of desert real estate at AMREP's Rio Rancho Estates, outside of Albuquerque, for $2,500—$260 down, $34 a month for seven years, sight unseen. Charlotte and her prospective client are not alone. The room is packed with sales people and freeloaders in small groups that constantly change as the AMREP representatives scramble for likely prospects. The guests, evidently drawn at random from the phone book, range from hippies to pensioners, of all colors, classes and ethnic accents. Whatever else it may be, AMREP is definitely an equal-opportunity outfit. The invitations to the "Gala New Mexico Dinner Reception" specify "couples only," to eliminate obvious no-sales. Still, no one checks marriage licenses, so a lot of singles come with friends just for the food. The guest list is small—perhaps 30 or fewer, divided into intimate, manageable groups. Each table is likely to include two uninitiated couples, as well as one couple that has bought land at a previous dinner and has been invited back to buy more, and to shill for AMREP. Each table is headed by a sales person, always referred to as a "land consultant."

To give the sales person a fighting chance against a tableful of total strangers, the first order of business is a seemingly innocent questionnaire. It asks, among other things:

1) Do you now have an income plan for your future?

2) What percent return are you receiving on your top investment?

3) If you were shown an investment program that consistently outperforms the above return, what amount could you set aside per month?

The questionnaire serves a double purpose. First, it gives the sales person the ammunition for the sales campaign to come and an estimate of the customer's potential. Second, it implants in the customer's mind the essential notion that "investment" is the main course at the dinner.

The before, during and after-dinner entertainment is a multi-media affair. There are slides, movies, brochures, charts, maps, platform talks and tête-à-têtes, as well as some planned spontaneous testimonials and demonstrations, all tending to induce in the guest the conviction that his destiny lies in a piece of New Mexico desert. The sales manager's opening remarks insistently repeat another key word, like a Pavlovian signal:

> . . . I welcome you now to join our very successful family of property owners, because certainly success does breed success, and there's absolutely nothing, but nothing, that succeeds like success. In that sense, I do wish each and every one of you success. . . .

This benediction is followed by allegations that Albuquerque is a city of cosmopolitan virtues: vibrant and modern, and at the same time romantic, old-world, and picturesque. Irradiated with healthful sunshine—"the climate is truly king . . . the sun shines 360 days a year"—New Mexico is a place "where millions of Americans are pouring in to enjoy longer . . . lives." (Exaggerated and unfounded health claims are not patented by AMREP. At a sales dinner in New York for General Development Corp., guests were told that moving to Florida's Gulf Coast would add more years to their lives than anything besides giving up cigarettes. Deming Ranchettes, in southwestern New Mexico, advertises unsubstantiated testimonials to remissions of symptoms, and to the claim that "hundreds have found relief here . . . from arthritis, sinus, asthma, and other respiratory disorders. . . .")

At Rio Rancho, AMREP's narrator goes on, "You can live like a king in God's country." The land consultant claims that "taxes are low because the state is so rich," and the state is so rich because "there is no welfare." Industry is booming—Albuquerque is the "electronics and research center of the country, and every other major type of industry is well represented"—so good jobs await immigrants. Indeed, because of its manifest and unlimited virtues, "Albuquerque has multiplied more than seven times in population in the last 35 years, and now stands on the threshhold of its greatest growth, with more people expected in the next ten years than in any similar period before."

But this good news, according to the pitch, entails a paradox. Over and over, in words and pictures, AMREP proclaims that Albuquerque, "bursting at the seams," has run out of room on the east side of the Rio Grande. On its eastern flank, growth is blocked by the Sandia Mountains; to the north, south and southwest by Indian reservations, government lands, Spanish land grants and other impediments. But, according to AMREP, this problem plays right into the pockets of profit-minded Rio Rancho landowners. Albuquerque, thus constricted, is doomed to absorb an additional 300,000 people in the imminent future, doubling its present size—and the only available living space lies to the northwest, across the Rio Grande, where Rio Rancho Estates ostensibly monopolizes the landscape. "Expansion is destined to take place in the general direction of Rio Rancho Estates," gloats AMREP. "Growth like this means more money in our pockets as landowners at Rio Rancho. . . ."

Vital access to the Rio Grande's west bank and Rio Rancho from Albuquerque is assured by new highways and bridges, no fewer than six of them, a film states. According to AMREP, this access is the guarantee of growth on the west bank. "This type of growth is what always happens when land is made accessible—whether it be New York's Verrazzano-Narrows Bridge that exploded land values in Staten Island, or the new bridges over the Rio Grande that are triggering the new growth on the West Side." AMREP's film, entitled "West Side Story," goes into raptures at the prospect: "The west side has been like a great force bottled in by a single valve, and the bridges are the gradual opening of this valve, allowing that great force to surge through." On the screen, a big red GROWTH arrow thrusts from the epicenter of an expanding Albuquerque toward the heart of Rio Rancho like a Panzer division blitzing through Belgium.

In fact, claims one lavish brochure, "if one accepts the predictions of the city fathers and population experts . . . that Albuquerque will have a population exceeding 600,000 by 1980 . . . then Rio Rancho Estates is virtually assured of becoming not only a sizeable 'sister city' but could even become the second largest city in the entire state!" The effect of such growth on land values at Rio Rancho is repeatedly spelled out: it is the quintessential ingredient in the speculative soufflé. "In the past 20 years," the dinner guest is told, "land prices in the Albuquerque area have increased at a rapid pace, averaging about 25 percent per year, but in many cases accelerating as much as 300 to 400 percent in a given year." Another version testifies that it is "typical for land values to jump 200 to 300 percent in a few short years."

The same kind of appreciation in land values is inevitable at Rio Rancho, especially because "within a year we'll be completely sold out," Charlotte warns her dinner companion. "Within a year, you'll have to go to the property owners to buy property, and pay five times the price for it. That's minimum. That's *minimum*. It goes up 12 percent at a shot, 15 percent. Constantly going up, and the reason people buy it here and now is that they're freezing it at today's price. . . ."

But even as the potential plutocrat is contemplating getting rich on his Rio Rancho investment, he is also being invited to move to Rio Rancho Estates, to exchange the pollution, crowding and crime of his urban prison for a life of relaxed comfort among the wonders of nature and good neighbors. He will "live like a king in God's country." Rio Rancho is no soulless, sprawling suburb, the sales manager proclaims, but "a brand new city that we're building from scratch . . . a real scientifically planned community . . . with all the shopping centers you need, the swim-cabana clubhouses, the houses of worship, the medical buildings, the golf courses, the motels, and of course a complete schooling system, from grade school through senior high school." The after-dinner film dotes on the opportunities for outdoor

living and recreation, featuring fishing and horse-
back riding along the banks of the clean, rushing Rio
Grande. With the charms of nearby Albuquerque,
the life-lengthening climate, and all the other advantages of the area, Rio Rancho is the best place for
the customer to while away a few short years waiting
for his investment to ripen.

In short, Rio Rancho Estates is a double-barrelled
blessing. The landowner can either live on his investment or cash it in, or both. How can he lose?
"Ladies and gentlemen," the sales manager explains,
"as well as being one of the finest areas in the world
to live in—and I couldn't wish anything better for
anyone—this is an investment program. This program has only one requirement: just keep an open
mind, because only an open mind can properly evaluate the extent and potential of the investment opportunity being offered to you here this evening . . . I
would like to repeat that word 'investment,' because
this is really the key, the theme, to our program.
Because we've come to the conclusion that whatever
your own personal aspirations, whatever they may
be—and I will assume that some of you may well be
thinking of retirement; others may be dreaming of
relocation—of course, ladies and gentlemen, aside
from relocation and retirement, I'm sure that everyone in this room would like to put themselves in a
position, through an investment program, where they
can accumulate the nest egg, the equity, for the
future years ahead. Let me assure you that any one
of the things that you are thinking about this evening can be accomplished through our investment
program."

In the event that the customer requires further assurance, however, he is offered convincing evidence of AMREP's corporate solidity: "The AMREP corporation happens to be a multimillion-dollar public corporation . . . with over $140 million in assets. . . . We are listed on the New York Stock Exchange. We do have thousands and thousands of shareholders to answer to." By the time the dinner comes to an end, the dessert is superfluous.

Meanwhile, back at the Rancho, things are not exactly as they have been represented in New York. For starters, the demographics projecting explosive population growth for Albuquerque—the key to Rio Rancho's investment value—are highly doubtful. In its statistics, AMREP has exaggerated the metropolitan area, which takes in all of Bernalillo County (pop. 350,000 according to AMREP, 315,774 according to the 1970 Census). Albuquerque proper's 1970 population is only 243,751. Since this real figure represents a population increase of only 20 percent or so for the decade 1960-70, there seems to be no justification for AMREP's projection of a population increase of 100 percent or more for the subsequent ten years—"more growth in the next ten years than in any ten years before." Only by reaching back for a base year to 1950—the start of Albuquerque's actual boom decade, which saw the population grow from 96,000 to 201,000—can AMREP justify an "increase of 240 percent," and even that figure seems to count the base population twice.

Still using the county population figures, Rio Rancho claims that Albuquerque is the "fourth fastest-growing U.S. city in the last 25 years," but

Bernalillo fails to appear on the U.S. Bureau of the Census list of the 25 fastest-growing counties in the decade 1960-70. Population predictions are a risky business at best, as recent revisions of national population projections have shown, and the Census Bureau has yet to come out with its 1980 hunches for the Albuquerque area. But it is certainly whimsical to expect, as AMREP's anonymous authorities do, that Albuquerque will reach anything like "600,000 by 1980," if ever. In fact, the official 1970 figures from the Bureau of the Census have nothing but bad news for Rio Rancho investors. In the decade 1960-1970, they report, the net in-migration to Bernalillo County—Albuquerque's metropolitan area—was "less than 0.05 percent." For neighboring Sandoval County, where Rio Rancho has been operating for a decade, the figures are even less encouraging: 270 more people moved out than moved in.

No one with any real concern for Albuquerque's well-being would hope for the kind of growth AMREP gloats about. The city's population explosion at mid-century was fueled by massive infusions of federal money, most of it for military research and bases. The result has been hardly the kind of peaceful, clean community AMREP pictures. The growth in Albuquerque's overall crime rate has kept pace with the population, until Albuquerque ranks number one on the FBI's list of crime-ridden cities for both 1971 and 1972, with almost six serious crimes per 100 residents. "When the population increases at the rate it did here, crime just seems to get out of hand," commented the Albuquerque Police Department to *The New Mexican*.

Even if Albuquerque keeps right on growing, there is no reason to believe, as AMREP would have it, that the city will reach either rapidly or slowly toward Rio Rancho Estates, raising the land values there. While it is true that there is a good deal of federal and state land around Albuquerque, there is also enough room within and close by the present city limits to accommodate any likely population growth for the foreseeable future. One city planner, surveying the city from the air, estimated that there were enough underdeveloped areas in the city's low-density sprawl to accommodate another 300,000 people. And an Albuquerque mortgage banker told a business friend in mid-1972 that there was then a glut of at least 3,000 brand-new rental units in just one section of town.

Even if the city should, by some miraculous population spurt, manage to jump its present limits, there is no reason to believe that it must head for Rio Rancho. Contrary to the impression given by AMREP's maps, Rio Rancho Estates is hardly the only subdivision on the perimeter of Albuquerque. For example, just south of Rio Rancho—and closer to downtown—is Horizon Corporation's 12,000-acre Paradise Hills, adjoined by the Falls Land and Development Co.'s Volcano Cliffs. To the north, there are Cochiti Lake's 7,500 acres of Indian land, giving the lie to AMREP's claim that reservations are forbidden to white neo-colonists. And near Belen, south of Albuquerque, Horizon has another 155,000 acres or so in several subdivisions. Indeed, according to an incomplete but conservative survey prepared by Gerald Roubal of the Middle Rio Grande Council of Governments, at last count Albuquerque was ringed by enough subdivision homesites to accommodate some 941,000 people—enough, just about, to double the population of the entire state. And it is the paranoid delusion of almost every one of these subdivisions that the City of Albuquerque is about to swallow it whole.

So the investment value of all those Rio Rancho lots unloaded on customers at land-sales dinners is, for all practical purposes, nil. Worse yet, with few exceptions, Rio Rancho lots cannot be resold at *any* price, nor is there any prospect of a market for them. In fact, while AMREP's sales people have been proclaiming that the grossly inflated land prices they have been quoting represent fair market value, the corporation has been whispering the truth in the pages of the legally required offering statement that most lot buyers evidently either do not read or fail to understand:

> . . . Lots may also be purchased for speculative purposes, but such purchasers are advised that resale for a profit may be difficult for a number of years in view of the fact that water and utilities may not be available to certain lots for an indefinite number of years; . . . and that in trying to make a resale the purchasers may be competing with the company, which has thousands of lots to sell.

Of course, the customer has to discover this admission for himself. He is not so "advised" by the sales person at his table, or by AMREP's films and printed material; all assure him of a speedy profit "in a few short years." He is not told that AMREP has already been selling Rio Rancho on this investment basis for ten years, with no demonstrable resale market in sight. Doubtless a few of the early takers, who bought lots in the initial Rio Rancho area for $1 down on a couple of hundred dollars have, after years of hardy pioneering, sold for more than they paid. But such technical winners are far outnumbered by the losers.

In reality, the would-be reseller is competing with more than AMREP. While Rio Rancho in 1972 was selling lots for as much as $5,000, one legitimate Albuquerque real-estate broker was offering 150 acres—including precious water rights and municipal services—in adjacent Corralles at half the rate. "Now some of this stuff, at $2,250 an acre and $1,750 an acre," the realtor reported, "is right across the fence from Rio Rancho, which is getting in the neighborhood of $2,500 a quarter-acre. So you can buy Corralles for seventeen-five, and you're having to pay $10,000 an acre right across the fence for Rio Rancho. You can buy the very nicest in Corralles for $10,000, and Rio Rancho's selling you desert for $10,000." On the question of resale, the same broker estimates that "under the Multiple Listing Service in the Albuquerque area, there must be 3,000 Rio Rancho lots for sale . . . by people from all over the country who want to get rid of their Rio Rancho property. 'Take over the payments' and this kind of stuff. They just want out of them." And despite assurances sales people have been known to give their customers that AMREP itself is about to go into the business of reselling lots on commission, there is no evidence

—much less any guarantee—that this is so. If it happens, it will be a first for the industry.

The simple fact is that the only value a Rio Rancho lot has, above the $25 at which it is assessed as grazing land, or the $125 or so AMREP bought it for, is what some city bumpkin who wouldn't know an acre from an anthill is willing to pay for it. And ironically, the higher the price, the more willing the customers. An ex-Horizon executive tells of a new Albuquerque subdivision: "Started at $600 a lot— couldn't sell it. Sixty days later, we raised the price to $800, then sixty days after that we raised it to $1,000 a lot. Then our pitch was really simple: 'Look, had you bought it four months ago, you'd have made four hundred bucks.' And then the sales really began to pick up."

And if Rio Rancho lots are outrageously oversold as investment properties, their suitability as homesteads—even allowing for differences in taste—is equally overstated. The gracious, spacious environment promised in the after-dinner film—"plenty of elbow room" for "Western-style living"—turns out in most cases to be an AMREP-designed-and-built variation on one of a dozen or so standard architectural themes, all managing to look alike under the superficial mock-adobe, pseudo-Spanish and other trims. The houses hew to a uniform building line, crowded by neighbors on either side of the narrow lots.

At Rio Rancho, the wide open spaces are strictly for salesmanship, and so are the half-acre lots. For when it actually comes to building a house at Rio Rancho, it matters not what lot the customer bought. It matters not that Charlotte at the Playboy Club dinner in New York insisted with flattering sincerity that "this is the half-acre you should take . . . this is a fantastic piece of property . . . I'm telling you something, this is an area when you went out and saw it you would be sorry you didn't buy three acres, you would be sorry you can't afford to buy ten acres—that's the kind of area."

The lot the customer buys is one thing; the lot he will build on is another. It will be in an area where AMREP has already invested in expensive services such as paved roads, curbs, pipes, wiring, and the rest. For AMREP, the return on that investment depends on how many homes can be built per foot of frontage: thus the narrow lots. So, exercising what AMREP touts at the dinner as an "exchange privilege," the customer will trade his half-acre of roomy desert wilderness for a house lot "of equal value" in a developed area.

Not "equal size," however: his building lot will be only half the size, or one-quarter acre, according to AMREP; and it will look even smaller hedged in by identical plots on all sides. In addition to the unequal trade, the customer will probably pay a cash differential in the bargain. There will be, first of all, the cost of improvements to consider. Then, too, the "value" of the land has doubtless increased since the customer bought his original lot, according to AMREP's practice of raising its prices. One aspiring home-builder complained to the Sandoval County commissioners that he was offered a homesite near —not adjoining—the golf course, in exchange for his original $2,700 half-acre plus $10,000.

In practical terms, it is difficult to distinguish between what AMREP whimsically calls its "exchange privilege" and what is more descriptively known in the hard-sell business as the "bait-and-switch" game. In this old con, the customer is lured into a deal by a low-price offer, only to find once he takes the bait that by one pretense or another he is making a more expensive purchase. A ruse by any other name. . . .

But at Rio Rancho, if the owner still insists on a full half-acre building site, AMREP will exile him to a dusty hilltop ghetto in the outback, accessible by unpaved road, served by individual septic tanks at the owner's expense and lacking many of the "improvements" available to other developed areas. In no case, however, will the customer who has been sold more than one lot on the premise that he is insuring his future privacy be allowed to build on a double site. His other lots will remain in the outback of Rio Rancho's 85,000 acres forever, gathering dust, waiting patiently to appreciate.

Even the best, most expensive, and most thoroughly developed areas at Rio Rancho, however, fail to live up to their billing as "a scientifically planned community," whatever that might be. Of the recreational complexes promised over dinner in New York —"as many as you would want"—there is only one, in the original developed area that AMREP uses as a sales showcase, and that one is considered by many present residents as "woefully inadequate." Rio Rancho's "houses of worship" cater to three faiths: non-denominational Christian, Baptist, and—promised soon—Church of God. There's nothing so kinky as a Catholic Church or a synagogue, though sales people reassure nervous Jewish prospects that Rio

Rancho is practically a kibbutz. For the first ten years of Rio Rancho, the "complete schooling system" consisted of the facilities in surrounding communities, to which Rio Rancho children were bused. Only recently has the city of Albuquerque built three temporary primary-school buildings at Rio Rancho and passed a bond issue for a proposed new high school, and there is still no sign of the rest of the system. One small shopping center is shared by the entire development. There is no movie theatre, no bowling alley, no shoemaker, no florist, no library, no public areas of any definition—none of a lot of things any planned community worthy of the name would certainly include from the start. Nor is there any attempt to create at Rio Rancho a system of interlocking but self-contained neighborhoods on a pedestrian scale, which are the basic modules of community life and the building blocks of serious planners. Instead, even with fewer than a thousand houses out of a potential 150,000 or so, Rio Rancho already suffers from endemic suburban sprawl.

The country club, one of AMREP's main selling points, is apparently quite satisfactory. It is not, however, available to Rio Rancho landowners as a function of their citizenship. Rather, Rio Rancho dwellers can frolic there for a fee—$250 initiation per family, plus $25 a month—just like anyone else. The "industrial area" that is pictured as the employer of many Rio Rancho citizens consists of a few small industries and one AMPEX plant, lured by AMREP with a gift of land. At this rate, there seems little chance that AMREP will ever be able to make good on its statement that Rio Rancho is already "well on its way to being self-sufficient," that there are plenty of jobs.

But from 1,800 miles away in New York, or in Chicago, or Buffalo, Rio Rancho's drawbacks are not readily apparent, especially in the glow of after-dinner when, following hard upon the ice cream, comes—the contract. In keeping with its policy of never calling anything by its rightful name, AMREP calls its contract a "Reservation and Purchase Agreement." Whatever it is called, though, the customer can hardly read it in the dim light. "There's nothing in this contract . . . that isn't for your benefit," soothes Charlotte, already filling in the numbers on the sextuplicate form. "It happens to have been made up by J. P. Rodgers, who's our Secretary of State." Charlotte's name-dropping is confused: in D.C. the Secretary of State was then *William* P. Rogers; in New York State, it was J. P. *Lomenzo.* In spite of its exalted origins, as claimed by Charlotte, the AMREP contract—typical of those in the subdivision business—is less than benign from the customer's point of view.

The customer agrees, after the down payment—AMREP likes to get 10 percent, to discourage easy defaults—to pay the balance of the purchase price in monthly installments, usually over seven years. To this balance, however, is added a 7½ percent "finance charge," although it is difficult to see that anything has been financed. AMREP has not loaned the customer any money. All the customer has is a hold on a piece of land to which he does not receive title, and in which he has no equity, until he completes his payments. The down payment—typically, $250 on a half-acre—probably more than covers AMREP's cost for the land. (Many subdividers operate under arrangements with the original landowners providing that they do not actually have to purchase the land until the title is passed.) The down payment also leaves room to cover AMREP's minimal development costs, which are almost nil on the vast unimproved areas of Rio Rancho, plus some of the sales expenses.

So the AMREP contract is not the purchase-money loan, or mortgage, that it seems to be. Rather, it is a standard installment-purchase contract, familiar in department-store charge accounts, except for the minor fact that the customer does not get the merchandise until it is all paid for, with interest. The "finance charge" is strictly a bonus for AMREP, then, a hidden charge added to the purchase price under an unassuming alias. The true standing of the "finance charge" is indicated in AMREP's annual financial statements. For the year ending April 30, 1971, for instance, AMREP reports "Interest income on homesite sales contracts" of $4,807,273; while AMREP's own interest payments, lumped under "Other expenses—Principally interest" are something less than $2,140,757. So AMREP can hardly claim that the "finance charge" is simply the cost of money being passed on to the customer.

The magnitude of the "finance charge" income in AMREP's financial picture is considerable. In fiscal 1971, AMREP's stated income from "homesite sales" —a whopping $44,806,840—included the total price of all lots sold during the period covered. According to AMREP, however, down payments averaged 11 percent of the total sales price, so the actual cash received from "sales" amounted to only something less than $5 million, plus the monthly installments from sales made in previous years. Against this much-diminished income, the "finance charge" bonus looms much larger.

AMREP holds no patent on this lucrative little device. Waxing expansive on the contribution its Palm Coast development would make to ITT's coffers, the head of the conglomerate's subdivision subsidiary told Alan Gersten of the *Miami News* in 1970: "You make some money on the sale itself and additional money from interest income, which is about 7 percent annually on the unpaid balance. That income is a significant part of the profit."

On the back of the contract—if he can read the fine, small print and decipher the legal language—the customer might learn that if he lapses in his installments he surrenders any rights he may have in the land, even if he is within a few months of the final payment. Everything he has already paid will be retained by Rio Rancho as "liquidated damages," and the land will revert to AMREP's inventory to be resold. Again, this is contrary to standard mortgage practice.

For his pledge to pay on schedule, the customer gets nothing in return beyond the promise that upon completion of payments he will receive a warranty deed to a designated piece of Rio Rancho desert. None of the development plans and amenities projected by AMREP in the sales presentation are included in the contract, nor are any of the verbal assurances made by the sales person. Indeed, the contract specifies that "no agent or representative of the Seller shall have any authority whatsoever to change or modify this Agreement in any manner, or to make any other agreement or representation on behalf of the Seller. . . ." The *hors d'oeuvres* are *hors de contract.*

Lest the customer, even after accepting AMREP's hospitality, balk at signing such a one-sided agreement, AMREP includes a feature designed to reassure even the most prudent: an apparent no-risk, money-back-if-not-completely-satisfied, guarantee. "Ladies and gentlemen," says the sales manager disarmingly, "we're not asking anyone in this room to take any chances at all with us. On the contrary, we're quite prepared to take all our chances with you. We're tying up very, very valuable property for six full months, giving you the opportunity to go to Albuquerque and Rio Rancho Estates. You use your own common sense, make your own decision. I don't think there's anything fairer in this world. And speaking of this world," he segues in perfect non-sequitur, "I know there are only two ways in this world to make money: one is of course to work for it—the other is to have it work for you."

The hitch is that in order to exercise this money-back guarantee the customer has to make what the contract calls a "registered personal inspection" of Rio Rancho Estates on a "Company-guided tour." On the tour, he will be submitted to five days of alternating good fellowship and hard-sell, in the company of 150 fellow soft-touches. Such conditions are hardly calculated to stiffen the customer's resistance, or to encourage a public change of heart—a confession, in effect, that he has been a boob.

Conveniently, AMREP offers its own package tour to Albuquerque from New York. The customers pay $435 per couple, which includes charter air fares, cut-rate meals, bus tours on AMREP buses, and group rates at motels of AMREP's choice (often its own). According to TWA—not AMREP's airline—a round-trip charter flight between New York and Albuquerque costs about $122.59 per seat, or $245 per couple, including first-class dinner and bar service but no movie. That leaves AMREP with something like $190 per couple to spend on turning its new customers into two-time losers. In its own defense, AMREP claims that the entire $435 is spent on "ground arrangements"—food, lodging, etc.—leaving the company to pick up the air fare, whatever it might be, as a loss, all in an effort to serve their customers. AMREP's itemized expense account includes $18.72 nightly per couple for motel accommodations. Howard Johnson's Motor Lodge offers a double room for $17.50 at full rate, while the new Hilton Inn in Albuquerque quotes $21; so it would be extravagant for AMREP to pay almost as much for its large group bookings guaranteed well in advance.

In the end, however, the chartered "inspection" tours yield a huge profit to AMREP. The truth is that these are not inspection tours for the customers' benefit at all, but "reload" opportunities, for AMREP's benefit. "Reloading" is the trade name for the practice of selling the same customer additional lots. It is standard practice in the land-sales business. Once a customer has proven susceptible to land fever, the theory goes, he is vulnerable to repeated attacks. It is a chronic disease, and there is no im-

munity from previous exposure. According to an ex-
executive at Horizon, "Seven days after a customer is
in, they start reloading him." He recalls one Horizon
charter from New York City to a Texas subdivision
that resulted in reloads worth $750,000, plus the
purchase of 23 houses. Similarly, Ben Hernandez, an
ex-New Mexico state legislator turned AMREP salesman, affirms that "they come in from New York with
a quarter of a million dollars worth of property, and
they'll leave with a million dollars worth of property."

In the interim between coming in and leaving,
AMREP's New York customer will be taken firmly
in tow—in one of the 125 radio-equipped, air-condi-
tioned cars in AMREP's fleet—by an on-site sales
person like Ben Hernandez. He will be taken on a
high-speed, hard-sell tour, leaving a plume of dust
behind as Hernandez pilots him up unpaved Progress Boulevard into the outback, referring casually
to one desolate, dusty crossroads as a future "freeway
intersection." On route, he will hear a reprise of
Charlotte's pitch in New York, with a few individual variations thrown in. "Two years from
now," Hernandez assures him, "if you have a half-
acre that you paid a thousand dollars for, and you
get a new buyer . . . he can't buy the land from us
. . . we'll sell him your half-acre at a much inflated
price—probably four, five thousand dollars for a
half-acre at that time, in two, three years. Your land
appreciates gradually, normally averaging 15 to 25
percent a year. We're coming to the last stages, which
means that your next appreciation will be a big one
. . . The price of a half-acre in Unit 26 [an especially
remote section of Rio Rancho] is $2,095 . . . From

what I've seen of Albuquerque, what I've seen of Rio Rancho, in through here by 1976-77 any half-acre can bring up to $7-9,000 . . . My advice is always buy before the price increases."

Waving a deprecating hand at the desert landscape, Hernandez advises the customer to "care less whether you get a pinon tree or whether it's a cactus. You are not buying trees or cactus, you're buying an investment, with most of the speculation gone out of it, because you have the trade-in right . . . People buy for three reasons: investment, investment, investment. The house is incidental. . . ."

In New York, with his "inspection tour" still in the future, the customer is offered further encouragement to trust AMREP. It is, after all, "a publicly held corporation with assets of over $140 million and tens of thousands of stockholders." A less flattering report in *The New Mexico Review* identifies AMREP as a recent descendant of a less-than-blue-chip outfit colorfully named the Great Sweet Grass Oils Company. Great Sweet Grass was a waterlogged stock offering sold to unwitting customers over the phone and through the mails from "boiler rooms" in New York, until the Securities and Exchange Commission lowered the boom. Its methods were strikingly similar to today's land-sale operations; only the merchandise was different. AMREP's legions of stockholders, according to Standard & Poor, are engaged in a high-risk speculation—though probably less so than AMREP's customers.

The land-sale dinner culminates in a moment of truth, after the films and the maps and the brochures, the small talk and the hype, when the customer and the "land consultant" come face to face over the contract. For the sales person, this crucial endgame has been analyzed and game-planned as thoroughly as a Bobby Fischer chess match. The good land hustler keeps constantly on the offensive. If the customer hesitates, the sales person insists that he confess his doubts. "What are you going to think about overnight?" Ben Hernandez asks an undecided prospect. "What's your problem? Tell me — right now." Charlotte, in New York, has the same strategy. "Now ask me some questions," she says. Once the sales person knows the customer's mind, he is back in control: for every objection, there is an appropriate response. If the customer continues to doubt, the onus is on him to call the sales person a liar to his face—this fellow human being with whom he has just sat down at table and broken bread, and exchanged friendly chitchat. So why not sign? "You're not committing yourself for anything," says Charlotte. The land consultant herself owns property. "I'm just working here so I can buy land," she says. Everyone buys land sight unseen. "This is the way you buy it. That's the way we sell it . . . That's the way everybody buys property. . . ."

3.
The selling
of the salesman

Only the most elaborate merchandising schemes include land-sales dinners. Less aggressive operators may simply wait in the boondocks for customers to walk in, attracted by nothing more than a billboard on the highway, or a newspaper or television advertisement. There are even some promotions that open with an ad and close by mail, with no personal contact. Demming Ranchettes promotes its $5-down, $5-a-month New Mexico wasteland with fanciful ads in everything from *TV Guide* to *The New York Times*. Responses are followed up with a more elaborate but no less fanciful brochure and an application form to be sent back with the down payment. With lots selling for $295 and $395, with $5 monthly payments, such a no-contact system works. Forbes Magazine's artfully understated appeals depend on the financial publisher's reputation for stuffy integrity and a single postcard view of its Sangre de Cristo subdivision in Colorado. A respondent receives a $5,000 contract with all the blanks already filled in—including the number of the lot that has been selected for him.

But in most cases, the sales person is the essential catalyst between a halfway unwilling customer and an altogether unlikely patch of land. Few subdivisions will willingly risk letting a prospective buyer onto the property for a look-see without a sales person at his elbow, like Virgil guiding Dante through the Inferno, to color the evidence of his own eyes.

An effective sales person—like his credulous customer—is partly born and partly made that way. The merely good ones are naturally gregarious types, anxious to please and to initiate the neophyte into the mysteries of real estate. The truly gifted land hustlers have, in addition, an extraordinary sensitivity to the prospect's desires, and a ready reservoir of sympathy for the common problems and frustrations of the common man. More important, as one virtuoso ex-salesman, now reformed, puts it, "These guys can sense a victim—they can sense a guy that has no sales resistance." But it is difficult to discern whether sales people are being artful or artless when they insist, as they frequently do, that their customers are their friends. One veteran salesman for General Development Corporation proudly displays his record of 13 years of selling. The same names reappear year after year as unfailing investors in each new project, without either the salesman or the customers being any the wiser after 13 years without a penny's profit; indeed, without a single resale.

In fact this same salesman is his own best customer, appearing in his own sales records, he happily claims, no fewer than five times. And it is difficult to doubt an enthusiastic saleslady at Cochiti Lake when she says, "The only reason I'm working here is so I can make enough money to buy land myself," and adds that "it's so nice to be a part of people's dreams." Irrepressible cynicism in response to such disarming confidences may be misplaced; seller and buyer may very well see each other with self-recognition: *"mon semblable, mon frère!"*

The experience of one major subdivider suggests that certain personality factors may be common to both effective sales people and vulnerable customers. According to a former executive in charge of training Horizon's sales people in Albuquerque, "They've gone into people's backgrounds, to find out what kind of people make the best salesmen. And believe it or not, male beauticians are fantastic land salesmen . . . ambulance drivers . . . cab drivers . . . hospital interns. And they've come to this conclusion—that people who are not afraid to *touch* other people make good salesmen, for some reason." Evidently, one soft touch responds to another.

By converting his sales people into true believers early in the game, the promoter reaps an easy extra dividend. Horizon's former sales executive recalls that "these young kids in sales class would get so enthused, we'd throw a contract at 'em, and we'd sell land right in class." Some subdividers evidently try to enforce such enthusiasm, pressing their recruits to prove their faith in the project they are about to sell.

In 1970, a woman who had completed the sales training course at Great Western United's Cochiti Lake,
between Albuquerque and Santa Fe, sued the developer, charging that Great Western had refused to
make her a sales representative unless she bought a
lot at Cochiti Lake.

M. Penn Phillips and Nathan K. Mendelsohn, the
original entrepreneurs at Cochiti Lake before they
sold out to Great Western, used their sales trainees
slightly differently at their earlier California City
subdivision. A would-be land hustler was required
to bring a "client" to the site and sell him a lot before
he got his salesman's stripes. According to one report,
as much as 75 percent of the land at California City
was being sold to sales trainees, their immediate families and friends.

The lesson for the subdividers is obvious: in recruiting sales people—as in selling lots and attracting
customers—quantity pays better than quality. "You
run body shops," says Horizon's ex-executive. "The
hell with it. If you take 10 kids into the class every
week in a city like Albuquerque, you're going to sell
a minimum of ten lots a week. Because what they're
going to do, they know at least one person they can
sit down—their father, mother, grandmother—and
sell them a lot. Very often that's all the kid sells. . . ."

Sooner or later most sales people learn the same
tricks of the trade, even the same stock phrases. "How
much can you afford to invest?" is a standard leading
question from California to New York; "The land
doubles in value on the average every five years"—
never "six" or "four"—echoes from New Mexico to
Florida.

Homogeneity among sales people is reinforced by the processes of recruiting and natural selection. Subdividers commonly advertise for new blood with appeals to salespeople with experience in used cars, pots and pans, bibles, and home repairs, thus transfusing the accumulated wisdom of those fast-buck specialties into the real-estate business. Once in, the salesman enjoys almost unlimited mobility. Subdivisions tend to cluster in vulnerable areas, and personnel can and do jump from one to another in search of a better deal, carrying their expertise with them. With the larger subdividers, a sales person can move around the country without changing employers. The sales person with an outstanding record of moving lots and getting good down payments is a likely candidate for promotion to a supervisory position, where he passes on his secrets of success in return for a percentage of his team's commissions. Subdivision companies have their own mobility as well, buying and selling each other, acquiring each other's projects, spinning off new ones, and passing personnel around in the process. One way or another, in the course of things the most effective hard-sell techniques tend to be refined and perpetuated.

Management also encourages standardization of the most unscrupulous gimmicks by setting performance quotas that reward productivity, with no questions asked. "You give a guy a projection he's got to meet," recalls the former Horizon trainer, "you don't fire him—he fires himself. Every once in a while, maybe one out of every thirty guys, you get a guy that can sell."

This picture of Horizon's high-pressure personnel

policies is confirmed in a statement volunteered to HUD by Charles Schoenecke, who identified himself as the former regional director of Horizon's training program in the Rocky Mountain region. Horizon's managers, Schoenecke testified,

> ... bragged of playing the numbers game with both the salesmen and the customers. With salesmen, their retention rate was 10 percent (50 men retained for every 500 trained each year). Hard, ruthless, inhuman drive demanding high-volume sales regardless of how they are made weeds out all honest and sincere men ... and you wind up with only the hard core who would sell their own mother down the river for a buck. ... The corporations can play the numbers game and get by. They play the numbers game with the salesmen, which result [sic] in only the con artists being able to stand the pressure. They play the numbers game with the customers, knowing that if they can get by with only one percent registering complaints, their overall sales are sufficiently great to justify the additional expense in making refunds or handling matters that come before the regulatory bodies.

Like legitimate corporations, some of the major subdividers climax the selection process with formal training courses. The budding hustlers emerge from "basic training" like marines from Parris Island, thoroughly indoctrinated in both the rationale of their profession and its tactics. Their education is conducted by veteran salesmen with legendary reputations for earning six-figure commissions year after year. Like the customer, the recruit is conditioned to salivate at the word "success." Indeed, the first phase of the training program is nothing less than the selling of the salesman, steeping him in the same gospel truths of the trade that he will later use to sell the customer. "A lot of this will be for your own benefit as well as the customers'," begins one class lecture.

Both the flavor and the content of the curriculum are revealed in a series of unauthorized tape recordings made at sales training sessions held by Boise Cascade between 1969 and 1971, before Boise retired from the subdivision business. The presumption that Boise's sales methods are typical of the industry is supported by the fact that the company became a major subdivider quite suddenly by buying up existing projects, acquiring in many cases their sales forces and managements at the same time.

The opening session is led by a Boise sales executive named Bob Baldwin. To whet his audience's appetite for the good news to come, he begins with some bad news:

> I'm concerned. . . . I'm truly concerned. Because here in this great land of ours with opportunities galore at our fingertips, we go through a 45-year working lifetime and we earn anywhere from over two hundred thousand to a million dollars in income in that lifetime, and yet, at age 65, 98 percent of us will still have to rely on someone else or keep working for a living. That means that only 2 percent of Americans at age 65

are completely financially independent.
Now I think something is wrong—I think
something is drastically wrong. . . . That
means that the wealth of the nation is held
in 2 percent of the people's hands and if you
wonder why the nation is going like it is,
just remember that 2 percent of the people
are guiding it, and if you think money
doesn't control things, then you are more
naive than I am, and I am pretty naive,
coming from Idaho. . . . I think that something has gone wrong, something is drastically wrong—something is being kept from
the American people.

In short, as any Marxist knows, the workers get
screwed in a capitalist society. Bob Baldwin is not
preaching revolution, however; instead he offers a
piece of the action. "I found out," he announces as
though he had just discovered the heliocentric universe, "that basically our whole society is geared
around *money*." (In dealing with salesmen as with
customers, the first rule of the game is KISS: Keep
It Simple, Stupid.) "It's of vital importance, and yet
we say, 'Oh gee, don't let money grab ahold of you.
Money will be your downfall.' Well, it will, but
money *itself* won't because there is not a thing wrong
with money. Because it has been consistently promised the righteous by the Christian God that 'if you
but be righteous, I will promise you prosperity.' So
there is not a thing wrong with trying to make
money. . . ."

With God's endorsement of his premise that the
doors to the castle of success are locked against the

working man and money is the key, Baldwin continues, "I have found that there are three basic ways
to make money in our society." (KISS again.) Each
of the first two—working for wages and going into
business—he dismisses: "We can write that way off
for most Americans to make more money, can't we?"

The conclusion follows by elimination, Q.E.D. "Do
you realize," Baldwin asks rhetorically, "that leaves
only one area left for you to make money . . . for
most Americans to make the money that they want
to make in their life, and that's the use of No. 3—the
use of money. And why don't they do it? Because
they never learned the secret of how to make money
make money for them. It seems like only 2 percent,
3 percent or 5 percent of people have that mastered,
and it goes over the heads of everybody else. And
so the working people of America just go right on
working. . . ."

Back to the Bible, for Baldwin's exegesis of the
Parable of the Talents. The story of the two resourceful servants who doubled the money their master
gave them, and the feckless one who merely kept
the capital intact, brings Baldwin right to the point
he has been aiming for all along. "They had to put
it to work, they had to put it in a position of growth,
they had to go out and have it make money!" he
flourishes, like a Baptist preacher thumping home a
lesson from scripture. "That's synonymous for something in our society. You know what it's synonymous
with? INVESTING! They had to go out and IN-
VEST it somewhere!"

But invest it where? "Wouldn't you want to invest
it in the safest place you knew at the greatest return?

Wouldn't you? ... Would you be satisfied for [sic] anything less than the best investment that you could find, with the least possibility of risk, that would give you the most return? ... Well, to do that, you're going to have to do something. You owe it to yourself to investigate all of the different investments that there are, to come up with that one investment that in your opinion stands head and shoulders above any other, the one investment that in your opinion will give you the greatest return with the least amount of risk. Right? Don't you owe this to yourself?

"If you've got the time and you've got the money, you'll do just that. You'll go to the stock market, the bond market, the commodity market, art, rare books, coins, real estate—anything that will appreciate in value. ...You'll investigate these, won't you, so that you can come up with the best one? Isn't this what would make sense to you? So if you've got the time and money you can do this."

You don't? As luck would have it, Bob Baldwin has a shortcut: "And this is something that my father taught me when he said, 'Bob, if you can just take counsel from the [voice of] experience, you can gain the knowledge of life without ever having to go through the experience of life.' We have to take advantage of what the experienced have learned so that we can take their knowledge without taking the time or effort to go through their experiences."

BALDWIN: What did Andrew Carnegie have to say?

TRAINEES (reading from visuals): Ninety percent of all millionaires became so through owning real estate.

BALDWIN: What did you say?

TRAINEES: Ninety percent of all millionaires became so through owning real estate.

BALDWIN: Ninety percent of all millionaires became so through owning real estate? *Wow!*

After leading his congregation through a long litany of such testimonials to the land-wealth connection, Baldwin gives a solo reading of "a poem by Henry Woodward entitled *I am Real Estate. . . .* I don't think you can read it too much. Every time I hear it again, I get all enthused. . . ."

I am the basis of all wealth, the heritage of the wise, the thrifty and the prudent.

I am the poor man's joy and comfort, the rich man's prize, the right hand of capital, the silent partner of many thousands of successful men.

I am the solace of the widow, the comfort of old age, the cornerstone of security against misfortune and want.

I am handed down to children through generations·as a thing of greatest worth.

I am the choicest fruit of toil. Credit respects me, and yet, I am humble.

I stand for every man, bidding him to know me for what I am and possess me.

I grow and increase in value through countless days.

Though I seem dormant, my worth increases, never failing, never ceasing, for time is my aid and population eats upon my gains.

Fire and elements I defy, for they cannot destroy me.

My possessors learn to believe in me. Invariably they become envied.

While all things wither and decay, I survive.

The thriftless speak ill of me, the charlatans of finance attack me, yet I am trustworthy, I am sound. Unfailingly I triumph, and my detractors are disproved.

Minerals and oils come from me. I am the producer of food, the basis for ships and factories, yes, the foundation of banks.

Yet I am so common that thousands unthinkingly and unknowingly pass me by.

Thus, real estate is not only the first resort of the rich, but the last resort of the common man against the machinations of those very same rich to keep him down. The wisdom of investment in land must be defended against not only the "thriftless"—who would pay any heed to their carping?—but also against the "charlatans of finance," presumably the selfsame Carnegie, Roosevelt, Field, Getty and Co. cited as paragons of economic wisdom just a moment before.

"I don't go to bankers to find out if I should go into an investment," testifies Bob Baldwin, "and I don't go to lawyers. I found out that they don't know much, and the same goes for other professional people, too. You wouldn't go to a doctor to find out how to fix the transmission in your car, and you wouldn't go to a garage mechanic to fix your plumbing, would you?

Why do you go to bankers and lawyers to find out if you should go into an investment? They don't know. We have to educate them."

Bankers and lawyers and the like, according to Baldwin, want to keep your money in their hands, so they can invest it in real estate for their own profit. So they might advise you to keep money in savings accounts, to be eaten away by inflation instead of fattening on the land. "I think it's a crying shame, and I think it's our own cotton-picking fault, and I think it's *your* cotton-picking fault, because you have let it happen. Do you know how you let it happen? Who is it that we allowed to come to you when you were in grade school to talk about money? Who was it who came down to talk to you? Banker Jones. Wasn't it the local banker who came to talk to you, to tell you how you got to put that money into savings, started brainwashing you from the beginning of school . . . and if it wasn't the local banker, wasn't it the local insurance agent that we let come into our school and talk to our children about the advantages of putting your money into an insurance policy? . . . And is it any wonder we're brainwashed from childhood right on up to save money so that you can be independent at 65—retire and not have to work? If you want to know why 90 percent or 95 percent of we Americans still have to work at age 65, this is still one of the biggest reasons, and I'll debate that right down to my toenails with anybody."

After an hour or more of tongue-dancing nimbly between the simple and the specious, Bob Baldwin has established the two points on which the subdivision promoters base their appeal, to both salesmen and customers. The first is that land investment is the secret of financial success. The second is that the secrets of land speculation are closely guarded by the traditional authorities on investment and finance, who conspire to protect their plutocracy. But their essential tool, Baldwin reveals, is "leverage," which is "like drawing interest on $5,000 in the bank with only $1,000 in it."

"For example," he explains, "if you had $10,000 and you could buy $100,000 worth of stock, whoopee. Great, right? That's a 1-to-10 leverage ratio. If your stock went up 10 percent a year, your return would be 10 times 10, or 100 percent. But unfortunately, you don't, and to the average guy, $10,000 will buy $10,000 worth of stock on a 1-to-1 leverage ratio, and if the stock goes up 10 percent, that's his return: 10 percent.

"You used to buy stock on a 1-to-10 leverage until the crash in '29, but that's one of the things that helped lead to the crash in '29, too, so you can't do that any more. But $10,000 will still buy $100,000 worth of land. . . ." (Boise Cascade's Baldwin omits mentioning that the promotional subdivision industry's temptingly low down payments—and no-questions-asked credit policies—encourage contract cancellations and defaults. Both contributed to the collapse of Boise's land-sales operation in 1972.)

Land values rise with proximity to industry, highways and recreation areas. The trick, according to Baldwin, is simply to apply leverage to the purchase of land in these prime areas before demand forces prices up—and then sit back and watch your investment grow. All that is necessary is "VISION, GUTS

and MONEY." The investor has to be able to anticipate imminent value in a piece of land most people
wouldn't appreciate. Next, he must have the courage
to make a decision on the spur of the moment. "If
you don't have GUTS, or the ability to make a decision today, today becomes yesterday and yesterday
is too late. The world is full of 'I could've, I should've,
I would've, but I didn't.' " Finally, he must have the
cash, "because you usually don't get it for free."

The progression from abstract first principles to
the point where the customer is confronted with a
choice from a stacked deck has taken an hour and a
half. "But as far as I'm concerned," Baldwin claims,
"80 to 90 percent of my work is done right now. All
I have to do is adapt what my company has to all
these things that I've been talking to you about. And
it makes sense, doesn't it? Do you feel that I know
what I'm talking about? Do I have your confidence?
Where is the salesman's barrier? Am I telling you
truthful things? Am I telling you things that upon
hearing it you know it's the truth? Even though you
might not have thought of it in that light, you knew
the minute you heard it that it's true, isn't it? And
you know that I'm talking for your benefit to make
you realize that there's certain things that you're
going to have to do, right? So where's the salesman's
barrier? As far as I'm concerned, I'm home free right
now.

"And what's more, I can use my presentation on
any project, can't I? I don't even have to change it
if I go from one project to another, because these
things are true regardless of who you come up
against. So they should be applicable to anything,

right? Or any project, or any company, as far as that goes."

In fact, the same syllogism is taught—explicitly and by suggestion—to salesmen and customers alike, wherever God's littlest acres are sold. Bob Baldwin preaches the fundamental gospel of the business, the canon of one true faith embraced by ITT and AMREP, Horizon and GAC, General Development and Great Western, from border to border and sea to shining sea. As Bob Baldwin assures his students, just before turning to the nuts-and-bolts of bringing the customer and the land together, there is "so much power in truth in this business that you never have to fabricate, or say something just for the sake of a sale. Because there's nothing more powerful or convincing or beautiful than the truth. . . ."

4.
Foreplays and endgames

After the salesman is educated in the theoretical underpinnings of his profession, his attention is turned to the practical business of getting the prospect's signature on the contract. Some of the methodology is not much more sinister than the ABC's of salesmanship which might be taught to any Avon Lady. In the second phase of Boise Cascade's training program, the sales person learns how to color and decorate land maps to emphasize the attractiveness of the subdivision (color it green) and its desirable proximity to interstate highways, population centers and recreation areas. He is advised to clip magazine articles—*U.S. News & World Report* is a favorite source—and send away for government publications that echo the subdividers' ballyhoo about inexorably escalating land values. The classroom work even includes a demonstration of how to organize the sales person's attaché case to provide instant access to a whole catalogue of supportive material to counter any question the customer might raise.

Sales recruits also learn the more subtle techniques of manipulating the customer into position for the *coup de grace*, the "close," when the contract is presented for signature. The manipulation begins even before the sales person walks through the prospect's door on a home sales call.

"We used to use the telephone," says Horizon's former man-in-Albuquerque: "I would set up an appointment for a salesman. He's supposed to be there at 4:30, but I sense from the telephone conversation that the customer isn't going to be there, but that she could be sold. At 4:00, I have one of the girls in the office call and say that we have an emergency message for the salesman and we can't reach him, but he's going to be at the customer's house in 30 minutes. 'When he gets there, tell him to call the office—it's urgent.' And the customer's sense of decency says, 'I can't leave—this guy's got an emergency message.'

"He walks in the house," the Horizon veteran continues, "and the customer will say, 'Let's sit over here,' and he'll say, 'No, let's not—let's sit over here.' And then he'll say, 'No, this isn't really right—let's go over to the dining table.' And the wife'll say, 'I've got some things on the dining table,' and he'll say, 'That's all right—I'll help you move them.' The idea is to try two or three things to see if you can manipulate these people. If you can't move them, even to the table, chances are you're not going to sell them anything. But if you can get those two or three things going for you, you've broken them."

With the house call in progress, the telephone comes into play again. "I'd show the customer two or three parcels of land—never more than that because we don't want to confuse him—and I'd say to him, 'Which one do you like?' And he'd say, 'This one.' I'd get up immediately, pick up the telephone, call Horizon long distance. I'd say, 'I've just sold Lot so-and-so,' give them his full name and the whole bit, and then I'd hang up and he'd say, 'But I didn't buy it!' So I'd say, 'But you told me you wanted it. Good Lord, I've already called long distance, I've had them take it off inventory. . . .'"

Boise Cascade's Bob Baldwin plays a slight variation on the same tune. "Right now I know what parcels to talk to you about," he says at the climax of his pitch. "Parcel 276, 281 and 285. Those are the three best parcels in the whole kit and caboodle, and I'd like to show you one of these. Now I know that these were available this afternoon, last time I checked on my list, but I'm not sure if they're available now. So I'm going to have to call into the office. I'd like to take one of them off the market so that when you get up there this weekend—what have you got on more important this weekend than coming up and looking at a piece of property that could mean a lot to your future? Huh? May I use your telephone?'

"So I go to the telephone and get the inventory control at the project and I'll say, 'Hello, Rudy, is parcel 276 still available?'

" 'No, that's sold.'

" 'Parcel 276 is already gone. Is 281 available?'

" 'No, that's sold too.'

" 'Is parcel 285 still available? Yes? O.K., let's take 285 off the market. Put a reservation on it for Mr. and Mrs. . . .' "

Such tactics hinge on getting the prospect into what one top Boise Cascade salesman calls "the box" —the situation that has no exit except the one the sales person wants him to take. "I feel that if you can master this, this one point, this box," he advises Boise's trainees, "it will help you tremendously in this business."

Maneuvering the prospect into the box is a matter of "setting the ground rules:"

Mr. So-and-so, I want to explain to you how Boise Cascade does business, and at the end, I want you to agree with me that it's a reasonable way to do business.

They want you to know everything about them: why they're in this business, where they are, why they selected that area, all the things that they're doing to this property. They want you to know everything before you come up there. . . .

I'll be laying out the cards here, and we'll see if we can play the game. Does that make any sense to you?

(Answer: That makes sense to me.)

The next thing I want you to know, Mr. Watts, is that I'm an expert on the prop-. erty. I've seen that property in the good weather, and I've seen it in the bad weather. I know that property like the back of my hand. For you to know the property as well as I do, you would have to spend at least twenty days there. And I want you to agree with me right now, in the comfort and privacy of your home, that you would have to have marbles in your head to pick out one [lot] better than I could. Doesn't that make sense to you?

(Answer: That makes sense to me.)

Great. Now if you like the story I'm going to be telling you, we're going to be talking about a date this weekend that could be the most important date you've made this year. I want to know now: what will you be doing this weekend that's more important than arranging for your future happiness and security? Nothing's more important than that, is there?

Now, let's see where I can fit you in here. I'm really busy this weekend, but I have . . . Saturday or Sunday, which is better for you?

How about Sunday—morning or afternoon? . . .

Thus, the customer responds reasonably to a series of seemingly reasonable questions, only to arrive at an unreasonable position. The salesman can use another device to assure that the prospect will keep the appointment he has just been "boxed" into. The salesman tells him that he cannot reserve the best piece of property that he has in mind for his inspection without a deposit. The deposit is $25 or $100, depending on what the salesman thinks he can get away with. But, he says, since he has just met the customer, he will give him an equal amount of cash in exchange for the customer's check, which will be used to make the reservation. In effect, no money has actually changed hands, so the customer feels secure. But the salesman knows that he has broken the customer's resistance just by getting him to write a check. The ritual of the mock transaction gives the customer confidence in the salesman, and reinforces the Sunday date. Says the salesman:

> This will enable me to do a better job for you, to hold off a piece of property that I feel at this very moment is more valuable than others. I gotta get my people the best property.... I am a professional in this business. . . . Does that make sense to you?
>
> Now, if you take that ride up to the property, and you see everything that you should see, and I answer all your questions . . . I want you to be prepared with a yes or no answer. Procrastination is the death of all of us. A man who can't make a decision can't do anything. I'll be giving you all the information, all that you would need to make an intelligent decision, to look over before you come up here. When you come up there, I want you to be prepared with a yes or no answer. Does that make any sense to you? Does that sound like a reasonable way to do business? . . .
>
> Fine, Mr. Watts.

All the seemingly casual, unexceptionable questions are really "tie downs" calculated to program the prospect to agree with the salesman. "After they agree to everything, it's all downhill after that. You've set the ground rules. I have found that if you don't have dough, you have no show. The test if you made a good presentation is if you walk away with a check—a $25 check, minimum. And I have found that about 95 percent of my customers that I have received a check from have shown up at the property."

Once the prospect is on the lot that has been selected for him, Bob Baldwin has another way to induce a seemingly innocent cash commitment. Baldwin takes a handful of coins from his pocket and casts them over the lot. He is "planting a money tree," he tells the prospect, alluding to the investment potential of the land, and he invites the prospect to throw a coin of his own, in the spirit of the game. "If he throws money on that property," Baldwin assures the trainees, "he's bought it."

The sales person also learns to estimate how much a potential buyer might be good for. Bob Baldwin asks his customers, "What could you comfortably afford to invest without knocking you out of the ball park?" AMREP asks the same thing in its pre-dinner questionnaire. "How much could you afford to set aside each month?" is a stock leading question throughout the industry. With this information, Baldwin advises his students to offer a deal comfortably below what the customer says he can afford. "Don't overload them," he warns, for a very good reason. "We don't want them to get in too deep here. Let them crawl before they walk and walk before they run."

Similarly, Horizon's ex-trainer recalls that if a potential customer told him, " 'Well, I do have some money and I am interested in land, but I can't afford more than $300 down,' I tell her we have something for $150 down. If she says 'Well, I don't have that much,' I'd say, 'But you told me you had $300!' " What makes people so vulnerable to this simple strategem, according to this veteran salesman, is that "everybody's going to lie to you . . . Most often, everybody wants you to believe they're much better off than they really are, that they can afford a hell of a lot more than they can really afford. And so, consequently, we used to always write a contract for about half of what they said they could afford."

But according to Baldwin, one of his Boise Cascade colleagues "goes in immediately talking about two, three, four parcels. He never thinks about one parcel. And if people can only afford one, boy do they feel lucky that they're getting away with just one. They really feel like they've gotten off the hook with just one parcel. But then, you keep talking two, three, four parcels, you'll start hitting that many. You'd be surprised how much money people have, you really will."

By this time, presumably, the customer is primed and positioned for the crucial endgame—the "close." In approaching the big payoff, "one of the most important things you can learn," according to another successful salesman, "is the use of the right vocabulary. Because people never want to *buy* anything—they've already bought too much. And they don't want to *sign* anything—they've been told all their lives to be careful what they sign. And *contracts*—

they've got to read every word and then doubt it. So get those words out of your mind, even when you're talking among yourselves.

"Don't ever say *sign*. Have people 'O.K.' it. When you get the deal all written up, you turn it around and ask the guy to 'O.K.' it. He'll be glad to 'O.K.' it, but he's not going to *sign* it.

"Never ask them to *buy* anything—it's an 'investment.' It's not a *down payment*—it's an 'initial investment.' It's not a *monthly payment*—God, people have monthly payments on everything: their home, the car, the refrigerator, the color TV—it's a 'monthly investment' into their 'land bank.' They love making deposits in a bank.

"It's not a *contract*—it's an 'option agreement.' They have an option, they say, 'Well gee, that's great, I can get out any time I want.' But if you ask them to sign a contract without seeing it, there's no way they'll do it, but if you ask them to O.K. an option agreement, they'll be glad to go along with you, they'll do that any time.

"It's really amazing, those little words that'll kill a sale for you immediately. And if you keep saying buy, buy, buy, they'll say, 'I don't want to buy anything; but if you keep saying 'invest, invest, invest,' *everybody* wants to invest, everybody's interested in making money. That's the great thing about this business—that everybody you talk to on the street is interested in making money. . . ."

The penultimate tactic is usually a "trial close," one or a series of matter-of-fact choice-questions which advance the sales process by simply assuming that the prospect is going to sign. "Let's see how this looks on paper," the sales person may say, filling in the numbers on the contract. "How do you spell your full name, sir?" and "Would this be in your name or both names?" and "What is your home address?" bring the prospect painlessly down to the bottom line without giving him any opportunity to demur. "Remember," one subdivider exhorts his sales people, "if he has let you fill out the agreement, *he has bought.*"

If the prospect balks, however, the sales person is taught a number of stratagems to get him to cross over to the promised land. The sales person is cautioned never to give up on a prospect as long as he can grasp at any excuse to keep the conversation open, counting on the prospect's resistance giving out before the salesman's store of reopening gambits. As the sales manual for the California City promotion begun by N. K. Mendelsohn put it, "Ninety percent of the people buy because they lack the courage to continue saying no. Thus, in our sales presentation . . . we are certainly going to use both persistence and persuasion. . . ."

The trick is not simply to rebut the customer's objections, but actually to elicit them; even to seem to agree with them in a disarming way, only to turn them around and overcome the customer on his own terms. Thus, "Every objection gets you closer to the final yes," according to a General Development Corporation sales-training manual, which fell into the hands of *The Stars and Stripes* reporters during their 1972 investigation of land-sales frauds.

"There must be some good reason why you're hesitating to go ahead now," the General Development salesman is instructed to offer at the first sign of resistance. "Do you mind if I ask what it is?" Here, again, the sales person can "set the ground rules": "Just supposing we could meet your conditions," he may ask, would the prospect then be interested? Or, more bluntly, "What would it take to convince you?"

A former salesman for GAC, the giant Florida subdivider, told *The Stars and Stripes* of a switch on this technique. "You pack up your kit, put on your hat and coat and walk dejectedly towards the door. Just before you reach for the doorknob, you turn and say to the customer, 'Gee, Mr. Customer, you know I've got to make a living for my family at this job. Could you do me a favor and tell me just where I made a mistake in trying to sell you tonight so I won't repeat it?' and when he tells you, you're right back in there pitching."

A more elaborate version of the same ploy is the "Benjamin Franklin." According to GAC's veteran, "The customer says, 'I want to think it over.' The salesman then says, 'I understand, Mr. Customer, how you feel. You remind me of a great American and founding father of our country who liked to deliberate carefully before making a decision. You know what Benjamin Franklin did, Mr. Customer, before making a decision? He took a piece of paper and drew a line down the middle. Now, on the one side of the line he put all the arguments against and on the other side all arguments for a decision. . . .'"

Emulating Benjamin Franklin, the sales person has the opportunity to reprise all his arguments, and to give them shape and substance by writing them down. The prospect, unprepared, is then challenged to formulate written challenges to the sales person's carefully rehearsed points. (Benjamin Franklin is only one of a number of celebrated names used to add class to this gambit. But GAC's choice is appropriate. According to historian Merrill Jensen, Franklin spent years of pre-Revolutionary effort lobbying in England for a proposed land speculation to be called Vandalia. No sooner had the Continental Congress opened session than Franklin was petitioning there in the same cause.)

With the customer's own admission of what stands between him and the contract, and his tacit agreement to sign if the obstacles that he has guilelessly identified are dissolved, the resourceful sales person is back in business armed with some new advantages. In his responses to the customer's objections, the sales person is cautioned by General Development that "it's a serious mistake to think that logic and reason will move the prospect's thinking in the direction we want it to go." In order to help the sales person avoid "logic and reason," some promoters provide their people with simple formulae.

At General Development, the ploy is reduced to five easy steps:

STEP ONE—Listen carefully to the objection. Encourage the prospect by both word and action to express himself fully.

STEP TWO—Before answering the objection, lower the prospect's resistance or reduce his hostility with a softening statement.

STEP THREE—Convert the objection to a question.

STEP FOUR—Answer the question calmly and confidently.

STEP FIVE—Ask a closing question.

Horizon Corporation has a similar primer on how to turn the reluctant customer around and let him sell himself. The technique is acronymed SATMC, pronounced "satmac."

S—Smile. A smile is disarming and shows that we are not concerned about the excuse.

A—Agree. This removes any possibility of any argumentative attitude.

T—Turn the excuse. Show the other side of the question.

M—More value and reasons to buy. This is one reason why we skip many points during our sales talks. We have many new things to go back to and show if he brings up some excuse for not buying at the close of the presentation.

C—Close differently. Ask for the order by using a new "choice" question. If you have already asked for the order by saying, "Which of these properties do you like?" this time you might ask, "Would it be convenient to send these payments before the 15th . . . or after?" Or, "How do you usually take care of things like this—cash or pay a little each month?"

Following its five-step outline, General Development suggests how the sales person can apply it to nine typical customer cavils. For instance, he is told to translate "I can't afford it" into "Why is it to your

advantage to join our program?" and to respond:
Mr. Jones, when you pay your bills every
month, does it ever seem to you as if you're
working for everyone except yourself? I'd
like to show you a group of figures that you
may find interesting. Let's assume that a
man has received his paycheck for the entire month and that he's writing out checks
to pay his bills. Eight days' pay is going to
the grocer, the butcher and the milkman.
Eight days' pay goes for the rent, lights and
heat. Three days' pay is going to the doctor, dentist and other professionals. Four
days' pay goes for clothing. Four days' pay
goes for cigarettes, recreation and luxuries.
Three days' pay goes towards his car.

Now, Mr. Jones, if you'll add these up,
you'll find that 30 days' income is used. If
you're lucky and the month has 31 days,
then you may save that extra day's income
for yourself. Now, my thought is this: instead of working for all these other people,
pay the one who's making all of this possible. Pay yourself and your family first.
Isn't that the main reason for working?
That's what our program tries to accomplish for you and your family.

In the same way, the customer's reluctant protest
that "I can't afford it" becomes an inviting "How can
your program help overcome my debts?"

Mr. Jones, I believe what you're saying
is, you would go ahead with our program if
you could afford it. Is that true, Mr. Jones?

(Yes.) Many people need a compulsory savings plan to help them with their future and many firms help their employees accomplish this. For example, Mr. Jones, what if your boss called you into his office tomorrow morning and told you he was very sorry but the company was going to cut your pay to the extent of one dollar a day. However, the company was prepared to do something with this money that would benefit you and your family. The company was going to purchase a homesite for you in a beautiful community in Florida that you could use for your retirement or eventually sell.

Tell me honestly, Mr. Jones, if your boss said that to you tomorrow, would you quit your job? Of course you wouldn't. Do you know what you'd do? You'd rush home to Mrs. Jones, filled with excitement and enthusiasm. You'd tell her what a wonderful new plan the company has for its employees. And that's exactly the opportunity you have tonight. But instead of you thanking your boss, it's your wife and children who will be thanking you.

If the prospect remains recalcitrant, insisting that he can't afford to buy, Horizon advises the sales person to become more aggressive. "If you did decide to make the program part of your investment portfolio, Mr. Jones, could the pennies a day make you a candidate for the County Poorhouse? Mrs. Jones, would it take the mustard off the hot dogs or the syrup off the pancakes?" At another project, the salesman compares the monthly installments to what the customer spends for lunch money. Then, rhapsodizing about the values of the investment he is offering, he asks, "Couldn't you afford to brown-bag it for a while?"

When the sales person is still unable to make the sale, a specialist known as a "hard closer," often the sales manager or a veteran hustler, may be called in for what is known in the trade as a "takeover." The "hard closer" dispenses with the niceties in favor of psychological arm-twisting. "We had some guys who just loved to muscle the customers," recalls Horizon's former sales-training executive. In earlier days of subdivision promotions, guests at sales dinners reportedly would be locked in until they signed. These days, a "hard closer" is more likely to cow the guest with: "You mean, you've eaten our food and you had no intention of buying? What kind of human being are you?"

Or, with the unwilling customer's wife present, the "hard closer" may accuse him of lacking a decent concern for the future financial security of his loved ones. He may wonder if the customer has the guts to make a decision, or the brains to know what's good for him. "You're just not smart enough," the sales person says in disgust. "We're not going to waste any more time—we're professionals." Alternatively, "A person would be stupid not to appreciate that," asserts a General Development Corp. salesman after making a particularly outrageous claim. "But we're not stupid, are we?"

One sales manager for Great Western United's

Cochiti Lake project between Albuquerque and Santa Fe mixes insult with flattery. After lowering the down payment on a $5,190 lot—one-seventh of an acre with a vertical slope—from $590 to $120, to no avail, he leans into his customer with the intensity of Billy Graham reaching for a sinner who is going down for the third time. "You know what the trouble with you is?" he demands. "The trouble with you is you're just like Einstein. Now Einstein, he was a genius. But Einstein, he could never make up his mind about anything. He had to think everything over from every angle before he made a decision. And you know something?" he concludes, driving the point home with a finger jabbing the tabletop. *"Einstein died so poor the state had to bury him."*

PART TWO

The
land lords

5.
Homes, homes on the range

The arithmetic of land subdivision in the Southwest is simple. It takes a couple of hundred acres of the arid semidesert to afford subsistence rations for one cow. Accordingly, large tracts of rangeland can be bought for as little as $100 or less per acre, and are commonly assessed at $25 per acre for tax purposes. But, cut up into quarter-acre lots and rebaptized Rio Paradiso Ranchettes, the same acre that barely supports one sirloin steak will provide ample range for four American families, who can be bamboozled into paying as much as $20,000 for the space.

As sure as the Southwestern sunshine, then, subdivision lots spring up faster than buffalo grass. According to the Arizona Department of Economic Planning and Development, that state already has 182 subdivisions of 640 acres (one square mile) or more, each at least three miles from the nearest incorporated area—out of the path of anticipated urban growth. These subdivisions alone, omitting the unknown number of smaller projects, cover more than a million acres, enough land for a minimum of 7.5 million people. Official projections, however, anticipate that Arizona will add only 2.5 million people in the next 25 years, most of them in the urban and suburban areas of Tucson and Phoenix. Meanwhile, the federal government's Office of Interstate Land Sales Registration lists a total of 460 subdivisions selling Arizona desert lots in interstate commerce.

Arizona is hardly alone. Just next door in New Mexico, with a present population of about 1 million people, it is estimated that more than 1 million vacant acres have already been subdivided, with no tenants in sight.

As fast as the surveyors can lay out straight lines on the seamless desert, additional subdivisions are platted to increase the existing surplus. As long ago as 1967, when the Bureau of the Census published its most recent count of vacant lots, Arizona and New Mexico had more than 250,000 between them—one-third of all the lots platted in the two states—and the total was rising fast. Throughout the Southwest, new promotions with their flashy billboards and imposing false fronts must now compete for space with ghost subdivisions which have not survived except as graveyards for disappointed dreams. Even the floor of Death Valley—120 degrees and no shade on a mild summer day—was sold off for house lots a century ago by an enterprising California hustler.

At a glance, the desert subdivisions seem to have little impact on the landscape. It is often impossible to tell without a map where a platted subdivision ends and open country begins. Like the reasons for platting and selling desert subdivisions in the first place, the considerations that delay widespread desecration of the desert are economic. Indeed, there are some subdividers who defer any disturbance to the surface of the land, not out of ecological fastidiousness, or love of beauty, or respect for the integrity of the desert environment, but rather out of respect for the fact that disturbing the land costs money. The true developer has to pay for bulldozers and trucks, architects and planners, asphalt and lumber. Most promoters prefer to save their money, so they opt to be nondevelopers.

In extreme cases, the result is a subdivision consisting wholly of a vast grid of bladed dirt roads, fronted by nothing more substantial than an elaborate sales campaign. Other subdividers splurge on showy roadside displays: an imposing stone entrance, perhaps a guardhouse to assure security, then a tree-lined avenue leading to an on-site sales office and a developed "core area." A real high-roller adorns his projects with promotable facilities such as a golf course, complete with country club and pro shop, an artificial lake, swimming pool, stables, and similar improvements, elaborate enough to be photogenic for the sales films and brochures, but totally inadequate to serve the population projected for the desert that stretches unimproved from the ninth green to the horizon.

For his self-serving virtue in leaving most of his

domain undisturbed, for the moment at least, the subdivider can reap a double reward. Because he does not actually deed the land to the lot buyer at the time of sale, promising only to turn over title when the installments are all paid 10 years later, the subdivider can in effect sell land he does not own. Instead of buying the land outright, he can negotiate an option allowing him to purchase the land only as the sales contracts mature. Meanwhile, the subdivider conserves capital, later buying the land with money that has in effect been loaned to him by the customer—with the lender paying interest instead of the borrower. The original landowner retains the use of a slowly declining portion of his land, while harvesting a cash dividend.

As an alternative to such delayed purchase arrangements, the promoter who acquires his entire acreage at the outset can continue to value all but his improved "core area" as agricultural land for the benefit of the tax assessor. Perhaps a nearby rancher will even run his herd on the property and pay the subdivider a fee. One way or the other, there are cattle grazing the outback at Rio Rancho Estates, and AMREP's salesman, Ben Hernandez, tells his prospects that they belong to Governor Bruce King, one of the land's former owners. While the land is taxed on its assessment as range—$25 an acre or so —AMREP is selling it as half-acre homesites for $6,000 and more an acre.

While saving the front-end costs of real development, the subdivider may also promote his reverence for the environment, offering unspoiled nature as a trendy selling point for the Ecology Generation.

Hardly a subdivider misses the opportunity to claim kinship with Henry David Thoreau and John Muir in the conservation brotherhood. "At each of our communities, we enhance and protect the natural beauty of the area," boasts GAC Properties, which has drained thousands of acres of Florida wetlands with almost 200 miles of dead-end canals at Cape Coral. "Palm Coast has been planned to save as much of the existing wooded areas as possible," claims ITT in a brochure testifying to its ecological *bona fides*, while admitting in its legally required offering statement that "until such time as Deeds are delivered, ITT Rayonier, Incorporated has the right to harvest all merchantable timber on the property" and leave the stumps for the lot buyer to remove at his own expense.

AMREP, which proposes to enforce suburban geometry on almost 150 square miles of New Mexican desert, beguiles prospects with the AMREP Pledge:

> AMREP Corporation pledges that its community development projects will be so planned and constructed as to preserve the natural beauty of their surroundings . . . with a generous balance of greensward and recreation areas, and with permanent safeguards against the blighting of the countryside. . . .
>
> This pledge is a commitment that all AMREP developments will emerge as communities enriched by the natural beauty of their environment, preserving for our descendants the purity of the sparkling

rivers and crystal lakes around us, and of
the air and sunshine above.

Unhappily, such marriages of convenience between
the entrepreneurs and the environment, enforced
more by economics than affection, are destined to
endure only as long as the promoter is selling the illusion of development in place of the reality, and
pocketing the difference. For just so long, the roadside billboards describing the wonders of Rancho
Paradiso or the Garden of Eden Estates will screen
nothing more than a few scattered houses or isolated
"core areas" waiting in the wind and the sun for the
"scientifically master-planned community" the promoter promised.

As long as the promoter defaults on those promises,
the desert continues to benefit from benign neglect.
The only major damage to the land—apart from the
esthetic blight of the billboards and a few split-level
dream houses—is the network of unpaved subdivision roads, required by some states to afford the customer technical access to his homestead. According
to one estimate, a single mile of dirt road, exposed
to the desert winds, can lose as much as 145 tons of
dust to the sky each year. Already, New Mexico alone
has some 8,000 miles of these roads adding the red
ocher of the desert palette to the Southwestern sunset. In the unhealing desert, even the most poorly
constructed subdivision road promises to be as persistent as the tracks of General Patton's World War
II tanks, still visible from his maneuvers in the California desert. From the air, the plat maps of decades-
old subdivisions can be seen etched large on the
landscape, as though some obsessed celestial geom-

eter had undertaken to rectify the terrain with linear grids.

In the desert, the greater hazard may not be the danger to the customer that his subdivision will never be developed, but the threat to land and landowner alike that it will. The subdivider almost certainly lacks any real commitment to the dream he sells, or the resources to make it a reality. And the original customer—and perhaps his heirs as well—may die or default while waiting for the millenium. But as long as a subdivision remains on the books at the county courthouse, there will always be the chance that it will attract some fortuitous development. Long before that never-never day when the project begins to look like its promoter's fanciful projection, the earlier pioneers of development in the subdivision will come hard up against the fundamental fact of all life in the desert: water.

•

6.
Making
the desert
bloom

People from places blessed by 30 or 50 or more inches of annual rain cannot comprehend the perpetual thirst of areas baptized by a scant eight inches or less. It is a subject for horse operas, in which a man's rights to his water are as good a reason for gunplay as his right to his woman. But throughout the bone-dry reaches of the Southwest, roasted by the ceaseless sun and fanned by the desiccating wind, water is closely rationed, dearly bought, and desperately contested.

According to official state statistics based on the period 1960-64, New Mexico has an annual surface-water income in its rivers, streams and lakes of 5.7 million acre-feet. (An acre-foot is the amount of water necessary to cover one acre of surface to a depth of one foot, or approximately 326,000 gallons.)

Of this gross income, 3.4 million acre-feet must flow
out of the state untouched to meet interstate and international water commitments, leaving 2.3 million
acre-feet for consumptive use in New Mexico. More
than 1.3 million acre-feet are simply lost, more or less
inevitably, by transpiration from vegetation, evapo-
ration, seepage, etc. This leaves only some 860,000
acre-feet for the discretionary use of the people of
the state.

All of the surface water in New Mexico has long
since been allocated, and the state is living above its
annual water income without adequate provision for
future concentrations of population, agriculture or
industry. Deficits in the surface-water budget are
made up by withdrawals from underground reserves
of fossil water, which are not readily recharged and
are therefore considered non-renewable resources.
Indeed, the state capital, Santa Fe, with a present
population of only 41,000, outgrew its surface-water
supply around 1880 and began a steadily growing
reliance on underground supplements.

Well over half of the state's present annual water
appetite is satisfied by fossil water. Fortunately, New
Mexico's underground fresh-water reserves total an
estimated 5 billion acre-feet: enough for 5,000 years
at the 1960-64 rate of consumption. But annual withdrawals on this reserve have been increasing year by
year due to growth in both population and per-
capita demand.

More important, the state's seemingly inexhausti-
ble underground-water resource is limited by local
geological and hydrological factors. Economically
recoverable ground water is not evenly distributed

throughout the state. Where it does exist, it often cannot be withdrawn without unacceptable consequences: the drying up of nearby wells, the intrusion of saline water into depleted aquifers, a general lowering of subsurface water levels. According to former New Mexico state hydrologist Zane Spiegel, the water table in areas south and west of Santa Fe has dropped 100 feet in recent years.

Other areas of the water-poor Southwest have seen their underground aquifers squeezed dry under the weight of insupportable development. In the report of a study group fielded by Ralph Nader:

> Former Secretary of Interior Stewart Udall observed that Southern California, West Texas, Colorado, and even his home state of Arizona have greatly depleted underground water supplies, as if water were an inexhaustible resource. In his view, the Arizona "water crisis" was "self-caused." As a result of the huge overdrafts, Arizona's groundwater bank account of 700 million acre-feet of economically recoverable water has dropped by 100 million acre-feet. Each year, water users withdraw 3.5 million acre-feet more than they return to the groundwater supply.

Chronic and increasingly severe water shortages in the Southwest have inspired recurring dreams of a Great Technological Fix—in this case, any of various schemes to divert water from elsewhere to the Southwest. One, the Bureau of Reclamation's Western U.S. Water Plan, seeks "the most acceptable means of augmenting the water supply of the Colorado River." The ultimate fantasy of such plans is to reach for the Columbia River, or even the Yukon, and drain them into the Colorado to flow through the Southwest, then Mexico, to the Pacific at Baja California. Such schemes are avidly supported by business interests, boosters, and their political hand-maidens. "Our best bet to provide a foundation for a new economy," former New Mexico Lieutenant Governor E. Lee Francis has stated, "is to move to-ward accomplishment of our 'Operation Water Wagon, which would make available to us water from Canada—the only abundant source on this hemisphere."

The reaction of our northerly neighbors to this proposed water grab has not yet been heard dis-tinctly, though it might be inferred from Canada's feisty attitude of late toward other American pro-posals, including the trans-Canada alternative to the Alaskan pipeline. Meanwhile, with regard to water, there are saner voices in the Lower 48. "I am con-strained to offer the observation," temporized New Mexico State Engineer Steven E. Reynolds, "that most of the sources of water listed for consideration . . . are in need of further basic and applied research and do not at this time provide a firm foundation for plans for augmentation."

A more deeply rooted objection to the Western U.S. Water Plan was reported from the Montana State Department of Fish and Game. According to the director of the Montana Water Resources Board:

> The State Department of Fish and Game
> does not agree that using human popula-
> tions to determine what the resource must

produce constitutes logical planning. Instead, it appears to them that an estimate of what the resources can produce must be used to determine at what point the human population must be limited in order to maintain the present level of satisfaction of individual "needs"; or, conversely, at what point each person's "needs" must be reduced in order to allow for a greater number of individuals. . . . The capacity of the land and water to produce the products necessary for a quality life for humans is a more important base for planning than is the capacity of humans to increase their numbers.

Meanwhile, in the absence of imported water, the rights to New Mexico's limited water supplies are regulated by constitutional principles elaborated in volumes of laws and regulations. In synopsis, the State Planning Office says:

Under this doctrine, one has no right to the use of water simply because it flows by or through or under his land. This is a practical system for management of water in an arid environment. Certainly development of any nature would be discouraged if it were possible for the latecomer to interfere in any way with water supply upon which earlier investments were made.

In short, it's a matter of first come, first served. Or, in water-law terminology, "prior beneficial use." Any new use of water from any water system in New Mexico is legally preceded by every existing use.

Under this system, the holder of low-priority water rights may have plenty of water in a wet year, or while the ground-water level is high. But in a dry year, he may have to let water flow untouched through his own property to satisfy some prior down-stream right, or dry up his own well so that the wells of previous users will flow. If a new user finds the available water rights insufficient for his needs, he may seek to purchase rights from someone else. The purchase of land alone doesn't necessarily mean much in New Mexico, unless it is accompanied by the purchase of water, and the water may more than double the price of the land.

Obviously, for the large-scale subdivider, a short-age of available water would be a disaster, at least to the extent that he really intends to develop his property. The problem is often avoided by shifting the responsibility for water to the individual lot owner, who enjoys a special exemption from the stric-tures of the water laws. Section 75-11-1 of the New Mexico Statutes requires the state engineer to issue a permit for an individual domestic well, which shall be allowed to draw up to three acre-feet of water per year. The law was intended to spare an individual home-builder a time-consuming, expensive and tor-tuous legal proceeding just to tap an insignificant amount of water.

In practice, however, Section 75-11-1 allows the subdivider to create an almost unlimited potential drain on water resources without paying for any more of it than he finds convenient. The subdivider may purchase water rights for the showcase facilities he installs to promote the project—the clubhouse and golf course, the sales office, the model homes. As homes are built, in tightly packed core areas dictated by the developer, additional water rights can be purchased by a utility set up and owned by the developer as a profitable sideline. Lot owners whom the utility cannot or will not service are assured of recourse to Section . 75-11-1, though they have no guarantee that individual wells will prove economically feasible, or even yield water at all.

Horizon Corporation, the largest of the Southwestern subdividers, holds more than 150,000 acres just south of Albuquerque. The nearest community is Belen, three miles away, with a population of 8,000. Horizon's project, broken up into Rio Grande Estates, Rancho Rio Grande, Enchanted Mesa and Rio Del Oro, theoretically could end up with a population of several hundred thousand people, becoming more than twice as large as Albuquerque itself. By the same token, Horizon could more than triple the Albuquerque area's water use, since relatively affluent suburbanites, with lawns and golf courses and dishwashers and daily showers, use more water per capita than the general population.

Nevertheless, in its legally required property report to the Office of Interstate Land Sales Registration, the only assurance Horizon offers is that "it is understood that the water supply is adequate to serve the anticipated population of the area." How or why "it is understood" is not spelled out in any more detail. There is no mention of any test wells to verify the availability of sufficient water. There is no demonstration that whatever water there is does not belong to someone else first; or that a couple of hundred thousand well pipes sucking away like so many soda straws in a glass of ice-cold Coke might not dry up some prior user's well.

In fact, Horizon offers only limited assurances that water will be available to any but a very few lots. "Water lines are extended to the lot line in Units 2 and 3 . . . these are now being installed in Unit 4." Beyond this, the buyer is on his own.

> *The developer makes no arrangements for the extension of these services to the other units or areas.* . . . Extensions of these to the user's property is available on an aid-in-construction basis, which is the user's advance of that part of the construction costs for line extensions from existing lines to the user's lot line which is in excess of that considered economically feasible by the utility. . . . Extension of these services to a particular lot . . . *may not be economically feasible for the lot owner.* . . . *There are no present plans for the water utility to serve the other units or areas* except for the Enchanted Mesa and Rio del Oro units. The owners in these other units or areas may drill domestic wells. The water table is 160 to 350 feet in depth and the costs of an individual well and pump run from $1,200 to $1,900. (emphasis added)

To the north of Albuquerque, AMREP's Rio Rancho Estates plays a similar semantic game with water availability. Here, too, the developer has installed water lines to supply the core area of tempting facilities and initial housing development. The water company is called the Albuquerque Utilities Corporation, described as "an affiliate of the developer." The developer, then, sells water to its land customers, at a basic monthly rate of $3.75 for the first 5,000 gallons—enough to drink, but not enough to make the desert lawn bloom. There is also a "hook-up charge of $350 for installation and connection of pipes from water main to house. . . ." The developer-owned utility also supplies water to support the greensward of the AMREP-owned golf course, the AMREP-owned motel, the community swimming pool, and other facilities that contribute to AMREP's cash flow and profits either directly through fees, rents, etc., or indirectly by adding credibility and glamour to the desert lots AMREP sells to the public.

Even though AMREP owns its own water utility, it does not guarantee water to the lots it sells. In its HUD property report, AMREP is allowed to state simply that "water is furnished . . . in portions of the residential areas in Units 11 and 16. The water company has *indicated* that it will expand its facilities to serve additional lots as and when houses are constructed thereon, *subject to its service extension policies. . . .*" (emphasis added) In response to HUD's question, "Will the water supply be adequate to serve the anticipated population of the area?", AMREP replies, "The developer believes that it will," and goes on to indicate that such supplies lie beneath the general area of Rio Rancho Estates in the sand-and-gravel Santa Fe Formation. In spite of its stated confidence that the water exists, AMREP does not specify that it has the right to tap into it, or that it has any binding intention of doing so in order to supply water to the 100,000 homes and more it expects its 85,000-plus acres at Rio Rancho eventually to accommodate.

AMREP's offering statement in the state of New York is a bit more specific than its property report to HUD, perhaps because New York State asks more specific questions than HUD. "At some future date, when and as the demand arises," the statement hedges, "the Utility Company intends to install additional distribution systems. . . . However, the possibility exists that no water service will be available to many of the lots for an indeterminate number of years. . . ." And then the bottom line: *"No representation or warranty is made that such service will ever be installed or rendered and lot purchasers should not rely on same when making a purchase."* (emphasis added)

Needless to say, such cautionary notes are never mentioned when Rio Rancho's sales force is selling the land. Customers who want to know about the possibility of building on their own lot, without exchanging it for a location where AMREP has installed services, may be told that they will have to dig their own well. They may or may not be told, as the offering statement cautions, that "due to the topography and the undulations of the property, the depth to which wells must be drilled are [sic] estimated to range from 400 to 700 feet. . . . While a lot owner may have an individual well drilled, costs of drilling a well for domestic purposes and having a tank and pump installed make individual wells impractical. . . ." Indeed, at a conservative rate of $6 a foot, an individual well at Rio Rancho would cost

between $2,400 and $4,200—as much as the lot, or
more—plus pump and tank.

Promoters who do not dress up their projects with
well-watered "front-end" showpieces—golf courses,
lawns, motels and swimming pools, and the like—
and who are not interested in fostering concentrations of early development in core areas, have it
easier even than AMREP and Horizon. They can
rely completely on the law requiring the state engineer to issue a permit for a single domestic well
drawing up to three acre-feet of water per year—
equal to 977,553 gallons—for household use, stock
watering, and limited non-commercial irrigation.

Select Western Lands, Inc., for instance, does business far from the relatively metropolitan exurbs of
Albuquerque, where Horizon and AMREP operate.
Select Western is in Luna County, in southwestern
New Mexico, near the small town of Deming. The
land around Deming was homesteaded in the first
decade of the twentieth century. A family then
could claim 160 acres by building a house, bringing
in a well, and cultivating a bit of the land. Today, a
latter-day homesteader pays $5 down—a third of the
price of a motel room for one night—against the full
purchase price of $299 for a "ranchette" at Select
Western's Sunshine Valley. For a dollar more down
and a dollar more a month, he get a $349 Deming
Ranchette from the same purveyors. There are no
amenities included in either deal, even for window
dressing. Select Western's development land actually
consists of 640-acre sections and pieces of sections
scattered all over the Luna County map; more a loose
confederation of small subdivisions than a develop-

ment, even in the pretentious sense that the word is commonly used. Moreover, Select Western is hardly the only "ranchette" rancher in Luna County. Deming Ranchettes and Sunshine Valley Ranchettes are indistinguishable from Enchanted Valley Estates or a host of other operations epicentered on Deming, population 8,500. And while Select Western's properties leapfrog south from Deming, other subdividers are pushing north from nearby Columbus, taking over the land section by section, dividing each 640-acre section not into four 160-acre quarters, as with the old homesteads, but into 1,280 half-acre "ranchettes."

A look at the landscape, the weather, and the location of Luna County explains why all but a very few of the tens and hundreds of thousands of subdivision lots in the area remain undeveloped, even years after their purchase—most often by mail order, sight unseen and no money back after 30 days if not completely satisfied. Still, there are enough lots—and enough of them sold—so that the traffic of visiting landowners is a significant factor in Deming's cotton and cattle economy. One would-be subdivider, defending the permissive local regulation of the industry, argued to the Luna County Commissioners: "Without subdivisions, Deming would be nothing. The only reason I have a good business is the people who come to Deming. Ranchette people have spent thousands of dollars in Deming. Why keep pushing them aside? These Ranchettes have made Deming. Any businessman can tell you that."

But, whereas buyers at higher-priced, more ambitious subdivisions might worry whether water from a central system will ever reach their lot, buyers of $349 Deming Ranchettes and the like are guaranteed that their only hope of water is to dig an individual well, at a cost conservatively estimated at more than $1,500—four times the cost of the lot. The developers boast that the use of irrigation water on nearby farms and cotton fields demonstrates the availability and quality of Deming water. "Its fertile soil and under-ground water await you," say the ads.

The advertising never bothers to point out that in the future, ranchette well-diggers will be competing with those very farms and cotton fields for the water of the Mimbres Valley Water Basin, which is under the protection of the state engineer. New Mexicans who have survived for generations on irrigation water are not placated by unsupported assurances from Horizon, AMREP, Select Western and other developers that their half-acre homesteaders can, without jeopardy, tap into plentiful ground-water reservoirs.

In July 1972 headlines in the *Albuquerque Journal* warned that "Lack of Rainfall May Halt Middle Rio Grande Irrigation." Though droughts are familiar occurrences in New Mexico, Dr. Bill Cody, chairman of the Middle Rio Grande Conservancy District, identified a new threat to the precarious water re-source. "I would say . . . that it may be soon that there won't be but a very little irrigated land in the Valley," he told a group of worried farmers in the Rio Grande Basin, which is four times as large as the Mimbres. "I feel that you soon are going to be com-peting with industry and municipal water systems to a degree that you will not be able to irrigate. . . . I don't like the idea of . . . city growth coming to the degree that we don't have any irrigated land, but I'm afraid it's coming. It may be closer than you think."

Select Western also makes a special point of the purity of its underlying water, echoing Deming's Chamber of Commerce boast of "AMERICA'S FINEST DRINKING WATER: 99.99% PURE." "Long ago," the sales material claims, "Government tests showed that the water which Deming drinks is America's finest." Whatever the source of this "long-ago" testimonial, it does not contemplate the effect on Deming's underground water supply of the new wells that will be withdrawing fresh water for human consumption, if any significant percentage of the available subdivision lots in the area are ever developed. Nor do the assurances of water purity anticipate an equal number of septic tanks close-ranked under the vast subdivision lands, percolating effluents back into the soil. Yet septic tanks, at $300 to $600 each, are the required means of disposal at the fancier developments of AMREP and Horizon, as well as at such no-frills, low-overhead operations as Select Western's.

AMREP, at least, did make an effort to improve its waste treatment—at taxpayers' expense. On April 23, 1971, Solomon H. Friend, AMREP's vice president and general counsel, addressed an appeal to William Ruckelshaus, then director of the Environmental Protection Agency in Washington. "Rio Rancho Estates is being developed," Mr. Friend opened, "with the hope and expectation that these purchasers over the next few years will relocate from the congested population centers to what is in effect a new community, providing employment opportunities and an improved quality of life and leisure." Thus allied with the government's interest in "new towns" and population dispersal, Mr. Friend went on to assure Mr. Ruckelshaus that ". . . our company has been committed to the building of this and similar communities in other parts of the country only in accordance with the highest standards of ecological and environmental excellence." He added:

Needless to say, Federal assistance would advance immeasurably both our ability and opportunity to provide the kind of community in which people will be proud and hope to live and will significantly advance the Government's policy of dispersing people from congested population centers into new communities.

Accordingly, we would appreciate any information you may have as to our company's eligibility for Federal assistance from the EPA for sewage treatment facilities or other utilities which bear upon creating and maintaining communities of high environmental and anti-pollution standards.

However, the reply from EPA's Office of Water Programs pointed out that EPA grants were made through the states, told Mr. Friend where to apply and enclosed an application blank. But a year later, AMREP was still advising that "sewage disposal facilities consist of individual septic tanks which are to be installed by the lot purchasers."

7.
Showdown at Santa Fe

The weight of the subdividers is felt not only on the traditional land-use patterns and water resources of an area, but on the political structure as well. Political power assures the promoter the necessary government approval for his subdivison in the first place. With enough leverage in the right places, he can arrange to have state and county roads built right up to the gate of his project, and even to have the local jurisdiction assume responsibility for the roads inside. The subdividers' political muscle in New Mexico has been strong enough to fight off determined attempts to pass unfriendly legislation. In 1972, the issue in dispute was the subdividers' beloved Section 75-11-1, which guarantees domestic well permits and allows the promoters to avoid the tiresome and expensive business of acquiring water rights for the entire subdivision at its inception.

A bill dealing specifically with subdivision water problems was before the thirtieth session of the New Mexico legislature, meeting in an abbreviated special session in January and February 1972. The legislation had been drafted in a series of inharmonious meetings between public-interest groups and subdividers. Observers at the private sessions reported that the question of water was the only subdivision problem the industry seemed even grudgingly willing to submit to legislation.

As drafted and introduced in the legislature, the bill limited water abuse at two stages of the subdivision process. First, it required the subdivider to demonstrate that water was available for the projected population before his plan could be approved. Projects within the state's declared water basins, where AMREP, Horizon and Select Western, among others, were already located, would be under the jurisdiction of the state engineer. Outside the declared basins, subdividers would be required to submit their own complete test data from a registered professional engineer to establish an adequate water resource. Water-quality and sewage-disposal plans would have to be approved by the director of the state Environmental Protection Agency. Until all these stipulations were met, the promoter would be prohibited from selling his lots.

At the same time, the bill specifically denied the subdividers recourse to Section 75-11-1. Because 75-11-1 grants permits for domestic wells without assurance that sufficient water is available, the denial of such permits protected lot buyers. And because

75-11-1 permits allocate water without reference to pre-existing uses, their denial protected the water supplies of established farmers and homesteaders. In short, the proposed legislation said no more than that subdividers could sell lots only if they had a demonstrable water resource that would not impinge on the supplies of those who got there first.

The legislation was recommended to the House and Senate by the governor, according to the law covering special sessions. It had widespread support in the legislature: the majority floor leader and the minority whip co-sponsored the bill in the House. Public-interest organizations supporting the bill included New Mexico Citizens for Clean Air and Water, the Sierra Club, the Citizens' Coalition For Land Use Planning, and the League of Women Voters. The Central Clearing House in Santa Fe, led by director Harvey Mudd and executive director Sally Rodgers, orchestrated the pro-control effort. Public-opinion polls showed a large majority of New Mexican citizens in favor of a legislative rein on the state's runaway subdivision boom.

No sooner was the legislation introduced in the House and Senate, however, than the pre-session accord between developers and anti-subdivision forces dissolved. The bill emerged from the House by a vote of 43 to 26, weakened by amendments but intact in its major provisions. Its backers hoped that the bill would be strengthened in the Senate; they were soon disappointed. An influential senator, Aubrey Dunn, maneuvered a substitute bill onto the floor, claiming that it would accomplish the same ends. The Dunn bill was in fact the mirror image of the original. The domestic-well permit under Section 75-11-1 was restored, and the authority of the state engineer to regulate water rights for subdivision lots was omitted. The Dunn bill did not deny permission to sell lots to subdivisions that threatened local water resources. Said the bill's sponsor, "I'm greatly concerned with New Mexico, and I'm concerned with forcing the little man out." Evidently, in Dunn's book the "little man" was the subdivider, not the customer. The opposition's attitude toward the latter was expressed by another senator, Eddie Barboa: "I don't see why we should spend hours worrying about somebody in New York spending $1,500 or $2,000 on a worthless piece of New Mexico land. If they're that stupid, let them do it."

After a third, compromise alternative was voted down, the proponents of effective subdivision legislation simply let the Dunn bill die. As one of the original bill's supporters said in the Senate of the Dunn substitute, "This bill has been called a tough bill by proponents, and . . . by the opponents a 'subdivider's bill.' It is neither. It is a nothing bill—full of sound and fury but signifying nothing. If it is so tough on subdivisions," the senator continued, "why has it been welcomed with open arms by subdividers? Not an iota of consumer protection is added by this bill."

"The subdividers' lobby is the strongest I've ever seen up here," reported Rep. James Koch of Santa Fe, who also complained that the developers "showed no willingness to work, compromise. . . ." Sally Rodgers, executive director of the Central Clearing House, charged that staff members were "threatened, offered bribes, intimidated, betrayed and made targets of smear tactics and personal attacks."

As it happened, the legislative session coincided with a strategically timed meeting in Santa Fe of the New Mexico Home Builders' Association, which perceived its best interests in the subdividers' camp. The builders threw a cocktail party at a local motel, to which all legislators were cordially invited. The guest list also included the major land-development companies. AMREP was represented by none other than vice president and general counsel Solomon H. Friend, the same Mr. Friend who showed such concern for water quality at Rio Rancho in his letter to William Ruckelshaus at EPA. Horizon's representative was Alfred J. Lehtonen, its vice president and chief legal talent, but until recently the federal official in charge of regulating interstate subdivision sales for the Department of Housing and Urban Development in Washington. Guests also came from Southwest Land Corporation, Great Western Cities, D. W. Falls, Sangre de Cristo, and other big subdividers.

The fraternity between politicians and land promoters in New Mexico is more than social. According to a report prepared by students at the University of New Mexico law school, "The major legislative opponents of the strong bills were in most cases easily identified with subdivider interests, and numerous serious problems of conflict of interest . . . were evident." Among the opponents of the strong subdivision bill were legislative alumni Carter Kirk, the "ranchette king" of Select Western Lands, a former assemblyman; and ex-senator Joe Skeen, who appeared before his former colleagues on behalf of the Southeast New Mexico Land Owners Association. There were also current members of the legislature with significant personal interests in land development and subdivision. Such conflicts of interest are not uncommon in Santa Fe. New Mexico maintains an amateur, part-time legislature, which normally meets for sixty days during odd-numbered years and for thirty days during even-numbered years. Members are paid $35.00 per day during the sessions. After expenses, then, they end up in the hole for the privilege of serving. The result is that legislators without independent means tend to have business interests that allow a month off each year for public-service power-brokering.

Among the participants in the legislative process with personal stakes in the outcome was Governor Bruce King himself. In partnership with his two brothers, Don and Sam, Governor King is reported to control close to half a million acres of New Mexico ranchland, which gives him an interest in common with those landowners who oppose subdivision control. Strong subdivision legislation, effectively barring the conversion of semi-arid rangeland into residential lots, could decrease the market value of the governor's holdings by hundreds of dollars per acre, and tens of millions of dollars all told.

During 1970 and 1971, while King was winning the Democratic primary and the gubernatorial election—on a platform including state-wide land-use planning—his King Brothers Ranch partnership was selling the eastern section of its Alamo Ranch north-

west of Albuquerque to AMREP, owners of the adjoining Rio Rancho Estates. The King land was sold
to AMREP in four parcels, ranging in size from
5,564 acres to 10,661 acres. The largest parcel was
traded in a three-way deal which gave the Kings'
land to AMREP; the 220,000-acre York Ranch south
of Albuquerque to the Kings; and the York family
more than $2 million in cash and notes. For the four
parcels, the King brothers reportedly got $7.1 mil-
lion. At the time they bought the Alamo Ranch,
before the subdivision boom began on the West
Mesa across the Rio Grande from Albuquerque,
rangeland reportedly was selling for fifty dollars an
acre or less. AMREP paid the Kings an estimated
$220 per acre.

While the King brothers' partnership has profitably sold land to AMREP in Albuquerque, the
governor's younger brother Don has influenced
AMREP's interests as the chairman of the Santa Fe
County Commission. Ten miles southeast of the New
Mexico capital, AMREP had ambitions to subdivide
a 27,000-acre ranch, purchased in 1969 for less than
$130 per acre, for resale as "Eldorado at Santa Fe."

The only obstacle was that in 1967 the county
commission, in response to earlier problems with
proliferating subdivisions, had set up a county planning commission. Even with a miserly $3,000 budget
and no powers to justify its title, the planning commission nonetheless provided a forum where questions about inappropriate subdivisions could be
heard and discussed. In the case of Eldorado, the
most important question was the same that was to
confront the 1972 legislative session: the availability

of enough water to satisfy the new demand.

On two separate occasions, Don King took advantage of his prerogative as chairman of the county commission to override the objections of planning commission members and approve both AMREP's master plan for the entire 27,000-acre development, and its application for an initial 6,000-acre subdivision. On the latter occasion, planning commission chairman Lewis Thompson asked for a delay so that the commission could have time to study the latest in a long series of water reports submitted by AMREP. When the request was brusquely ignored by Don King, Thompson and another member of the planning commission resigned in protest. "From my experience over the past several months," he said, "it appears that Santa Fe county planning is being conducted for the benefit of developers and not in the best interests of the citizens of Santa Fe. I believe that great and lasting harm could result from exercising a premature judgment at this time."

Governor King and brother Don were far from the only New Mexico political figures with close business ties to the subdividers, however. The name Montoya looms large in New Mexico politics: U.S. Senator Joseph M. Montoya; state Senator A. T. Montoya; Tom Montoya, one of three commissioners from Sandoval County, where AMREP's Rio Rancho Estates dominates the landscape and the politics. Theodore R. ("Ted") Montoya and his brother A. T. are partners in the law firm of Montoya & Montoya, AMREP's attorneys, with offices conveniently located at Rio Rancho Estates. It is said in New Mexico that subdivision legislation is written

in the offices of Montoya & Montoya, and though
A. T. Montoya fastidiously refrained from voting on
the 1972 bill in the legislature because of "certain
interests," his considerable political weight was felt
in Santa Fe.

"It is my firm belief," charged Harvey Mudd of
the Central Clearing House, "that it was the Montoya influence that killed the subdivision water-
conservation bill in the New Mexico Senate. Even
though Senator A. T. Montoya did not himself vote
on the bill, the influence of the Montoya machine
was far-reaching."

To which Senator A. T. Montoya replied: "I shook
hands with him and his hand was smaller than a
woman's hand, and I do not do business with a hand
that small. Next time I won't be so kind as to not
participate in the debate and the vote."

State Representative Turner Branch of Bernalillo
dispensed with the niceties the first time around.
Although he serves as attorney for Horizon, the
largest subdivider in New Mexico, with 175,000
acres, Rep. Branch voted for several weakening
amendments to the original subdivision legislation.
State Senator Edmundo Delgado also voted consistently against meaningful subdivision control while
serving as advertising agent for a development called
Colonias de Santa Fe.

The only result of the battle over subdivision control in New Mexico's thirtieth legislature was an
order from Governor King to the state's Environmental Improvement Board to form a special task
force to write a subdivision bill for consideration
by the thirty-first legislature. Among the members

of the board were George Labert, a vice president
of the Falls Land and Development Corp., and
Kenneth Brown, who practices law in the offices of
Montoya & Montoya.

The bill written by the land-subdivision task
force and enacted by the legislature in early 1973
held no pleasant surprises for the proponents of
strong subdivision control in New Mexico. The new
law vests all power to control subdivisions in the
state's 32 county commissions, each of which will
draw up its own regulations. In the past, the legislation's critics point out, many of these same county
commissions have demonstrated their willingness to
go along with even the most careless subdivision
schemes. The new law merely requires responsible
state agencies to "consult" with the county commissions on subdivision questions, and requires the commissions in turn to "consider" the advice they receive, but not necessarily to follow it. Violation of
the subdivision law is reduced from a felony with a
possible fine of $100,000 to a misdemeanor.

Attempts by the pro-control forces, led by the
Central Clearing House, to re-introduce legislation
banning 75-11-1 domestic-well permits in subdivisions were met with threats from the developers
that such a move would mean the defeat of any
subdivision legislation at all. The law the anti-sub-
dividers settled for means that promoters looking for
a likely site for another Rio Rancho or Deming
Ranchettes can still shop around among New Mexico's 32 counties until they find a compliant commission. Existing subdivisions—a million acres or more
of them—are unaffected by the new law.

8.
Giving it
to the Indians

Competition for New Mexico's water is complicated
by the prior claims of the Indian pueblos clustered
along the Rio Grande. Even when the Rio Grande is
flowing, which is not a guaranteed state of affairs, the
pueblos' proximity to the river does not confer on
them an unlimited and uncontested right to tap it.
On the one hand, there is reportedly a suppressed
Bureau of Indian Affairs study concluding that "the
blasted Indians own every blasted drop." But the
state of New Mexico, on the other hand, adamantly
maintains that it has the right to allocate water to
the pueblos according to the doctrine of "beneficial
use."

The conflict between the Indians' theoretical
water rights and New Mexico's water law has become more urgent as the subdividers have begun

to spread out along the Rio Grande generally, and on the Indian reservations in particular. With the outcome in doubt, occasional rivalries have arisen between pueblos with potentially competing claims to the life-giving Rio Grande. The Santo Domingo Pueblo, for instance, adjoins the pueblo of the Cochiti tribe, which has leased a large portion of its land for subdivision by the Great Western United conglomerate. The council of the Santo Domingos, alarmed at the threat of urban development representing a beneficial-use claim to the limited available water, is seeking to protect its own claims by plowing long-fallow Santo Domingo land.

The intrusion of white-owned subdivisions on the Indian reservations violates the commonly held belief that Indian lands are protected by the federal government against outside commercial exploitation. Rio Rancho Estates, for one, refers to this accepted principle to assure its customers that the Indian reservations preclude development anywhere in the Albuquerque area except at Rio Rancho. In fact, however, the sanctity of Indian lands is often honored in the breach. Every once in a while, as the spirit moves them, the Great White Fathers in Washington rediscover the potential virtues of reservation life, and the actual plight of reservation Indians. The preferred medicine to promote the viability of the Indians' appointed homelands is to invite white technology and expertise to participate in commercial development on the reservations. By some coincidence, however, such measures often give the white man access to untapped Indian resources at the very time the American economy has an appetite for them. The most recent case in point is the opening up to strip-mining of vast coalfields on the Hopi's sacred Black Mesa in Arizona, the Navajo reservation in northwest New Mexico, and the Northern Cheyenne domain in Montana.

The federal General Leasing Act of 1955 made the reservations vulnerable to "recreational" real-estate development by non-Indians. To the subdividers, the pueblos clustered along the Rio Grande are especially attractive. The Indians' legally guaranteed dominion over the reservations eliminates the tedious, expensive business of land acquisition from individual private landowners. The restriction of Indian land to long-term leases rather than outright purchase avoids the expense of fee-simple ownership. The Albuquerque-to-Sante Fe interstate parallels the Rio Grande, making the reservations potential bedroom suburbs and offering customers access to civilization as a counterpoint to the romance of living in luxury among authentic American primitives.

The subdivision at Cochiti Pueblo was specifically authorized by Public Law 90-570, a 1968 amendment to the 1955 Leasing Act, providing that reservation land could be leased to outside developers for 99 years. Accordingly, a lease between the Cochiti tribe and what is now the Great Western United conglomerate was signed in April 1969. Robert Bennett, the Bureau of Indian Affairs commissioner at the time, recalls that the government considered sponsoring one of three arrangements between the Indians and outside developers. The first scheme would have given the developer complete control over the project under a long-term lease from the tribe. The second would have allowed the Indians to develop the reservation land themselves, with mortgage financing secured by their land. The third arrangement envisioned joint ventures between the Indians and outside developers, with the Indians' land counting as their share of the investment capital.

Clearly, the last two alternatives promised the greatest benefits to the Indians from any successful commercial development on their reservations. The second alternative would have made the Indians the proprietors of their own enterprise, and the third would have had such ancillary benefits as the opportunity to develop managerial, sales and other professional skills among members of the tribe. By the same token, such arrangements might have afforded the Cochiti a heightened sense of dignity, of being in control once again of their own destiny, or at least part of it.

On the other hand, there were obvious obstacles to Indian ownership of whatever development might be established on their land. For all the obvious reasons of cultural differences and a century or more of discrimination, Indians as a group are short on the sophisticated skills necessary in a commercial venture of such size. In the case of the Cochitis, only 418 members of the tribe are currently accounted for on the reservation, and perhaps another 400 or so are living outside—hardly enough of a population pool from which to draw the necessary talent, even if it included a high percentage of Harvard Business School grads instead of old people and children, many of them illiterate or semi-literate in English and uncomfortable with the white man's ways. The subdivision that Great Western has been selling on the Cochiti land is intended to house 44,000 people, hardly any of them Indians.

The only way the Indians could have handled Scheme Two—development by themselves—would probably have been to hire outside professionals on a fee basis. The third alternative—a joint venture with a non-Indian partner—would seem to have offered the Indians the most help combined with the most benefit. According to BIA commissioner Bennett, however, the Cochiti leadership was "apprehensive about management." The BIA-sponsored choice: Scheme One. The Cochiti would simply lease their land—7,500 acres, almost a third of the reservation—to Great Western. In return, the Indians got a fixed percentage of Great Western's income from subleases and vague assurances that Indians would be hired for as many jobs as possible.

But before Great Western would consider a subdivision on Cochiti land, there had to be a Cochiti Lake to make the subdivision unique in an area where the forces of geology and meteorology conspire against standing bodies of water. "Cochiti Lake will be the only major body of water in this area," boasts a Great Western invitation to "add Cochiti Lake real-estate to your investment program! . . . In fact, it will be the only lake of any size within 100 miles." To make Great Western's boast come true, the Army Corps of Engineers is building a dam at the confluence of the Rio Grande and Santa Fe rivers to transform a narrow, steep desert valley into Cochiti Lake.

The projected cost of the five miles of earthfill, 251 feet above the river, is $82 million, charged to the U.S. taxpayer. Over the 99-year term of Great Western's lease with the Cochiti, which coincides conveniently with the Corps of Engineers' estimate of 100 years of useful life for the dam, that amounts to an $820,000 annual subsidy from the taxpayers to Great Western for the enhancement of their subdivision. As one salesman assured a reluctant investor, "that $82 million is what's making the value of your land go up."

It will take more than $82 million worth of earthmoving to make the Cochitis landlords to 44,000 palefaces in a subdivision about the size of Santa Fe. In one of its prepared sales pitches, Great Western claims that "the Bureau of Land Management, the Department of the Interior, the Bureau of Indian Affairs, the Army Corps of Engineers," assisted by Great Western Cities and the Cochitis, "have planned this community together and are working on it as a team." While this name-dropping exaggerates the government's participation, it is clearly true that the Department of the Interior, through its Bureau of Indian Affairs, stands as a de facto cosponsor of whatever results from the alliance between the Cochiti and their Great Western friends. In addition, it required the active collaboration of the Congress to provide the water that made it all possible.

The original plans formulated by the Corps of Engineers in the late 1940's and early 1950's for flood control in the Rio Grande Basin did not include a dam across the river at Cochiti. Indeed, because of opposition from New Mexico's neighbors, Colorado and Texas, both fearful that such dams would infringe upon their guaranteed water rights, any dam across the main stream of the Rio Grande was then politically impossible. The original plan was to control the flow of the main river by a series of smaller dams on its tributary streams.

By the time of the Flood Control Act of 1960, however, a flood-control dam was included at Cochiti, in response to persistent lobbying by development-minded business interests in the burgeoning Albuquerque-Santa Fe area. (In the previous two decades, Albuquerque had grown from 35,000 to 200,000 people, financed by massive investments of military and space money from Washington.) Flood control would be enhanced by water storage and recreation developments. Out of deference to the prior claims of Texas and Colorado, however, the 1960 act specified that the dam could not permanently retain any water from the Rio Grande. By requiring the annual release of stored flood waters, which would turn the dam's reservoir into a mudhole, the legislation precluded any recreation-based subdivision at Cochiti Lake as completely as though there had been no dam at all.

But the way around this obstacle was already at hand. The Bureau of Reclamation proposed to divert some of the 235,000 acre-feet of water a year due New Mexico from the San Juan River Basin—part of the Colorado River system to the northeast—into the Rio Grande Basin. The only obstacle to the San Juan interbasin transfer, however, was not legal but physical: the river basins are separated by the Continental Divide on the crest of the Rockies. Over or under, San Juan water had to cross the mountains. The choice was to tunnel for 13 miles beneath the mountains and turn the San Juan water into the Chama River, a Rio Grande tributary, at a cost of $84.5 million.

Of the 110,000 acre-feet added to the Rio Grande by the San Juan-Chama project, fully one half was tagged for delivery to Albuquerque for supposed industrial and municipal needs, almost doubling the city's 1970 water consumption level. It soon became apparent, however, that the city of Albuquerque had no real use for the additional water. "Albuquerque's share is bonus water really," boasted a promotional blurb from Rio Rancho Estates, which also stood to benefit from a lake, "since of all the cities in the semi-arid Southwest, Albuquerque has the most water. The city sits atop a one-mile deep, seven-mile wide water table which has been traditionally stable." The potential value of the redundant water, transported for hundreds of miles at public expense, was not lost on Rio Rancho's promoters: "The project will create several new lakes including one 22 miles north of Rio Rancho Estates. . . . Rio Rancho's varied recreational activities will be expanded to stress water sports." And, though Rio Rancho neglected to mention it, the lake 22 miles north of Rio Rancho would be right at Cochiti City.

But the San Juan Diversion Project legislation, passed by Congress in 1962, specifically limited the recreational uses of the water, and reinstated the prohibition against any main-stream dams on the Rio Grande to impound the augmented flow.

So, the 1960 Flood Control Act had authorized the dam but forbidden the permanent pooling of Rio Grande water; while the 1962 San Juan-Chama project legislation delivered non-Rio Grande water but forbade any dams. It remained for a third act of Congress, a 1964 amendment to the 1960 Flood Control Act—introduced by New Mexico's own congressman —finally to authorize a lake at Cochiti. The U.S. taxpayers would pick up the bill for the recreational water, as well as the dam.

According to Sam Arquero, governor of the Cochiti Pueblo, "the people"— meaning, of course, the Indians—"always objected to a dam" on the reservation. In all the deliberations, planning and legislative machinations that went into creating the project, the Cochiti were hardly consulted. Nevertheless, under threat of condemnation, the tribe allowed the Corps of Engineers to make tests to determine the feasibility of a dam at Cochiti as early as 1952. A 1926 act of Congress states that "lands of the Pueblo Indians of New Mexico, the Indian title to which has not been extinguished, may be condemned for any public purpose. . . ." "We were afraid they might condemn the area and we would be left without anything," said Governor Arquero.

With that inducement, the Cochiti entered into negotiations with the Corps of Engineers for an easement on the pueblo land to be occupied by the dam and reservoir. A May 24, 1964, resolution of the tribal council clearly indicates that the Indians were aware by then of the inevitability of the development and the extent of their loss:

WHEREAS, the Pueblo of Cochiti . . . has

been advised by the Corps of Engineers of
the United States Department of Defense
... that it is proposing to construct, operate and maintain a flood-control structure
on the Rio Grande near Cochiti Pueblo ... ;
and

WHEREAS, legislation has been
adopted which will authorize the Secretary
of the Interior to make water available for
a permanent pool for recreational purposes;
and

WHEREAS, the proposed dam and reservoir, when constructed, will occupy and
flood a large portion of the Pueblo lands;
and

WHEREAS, certain of the Pueblo lands
to be so occupied and inundated comprise
a substantial portion of the irrigated and
grazing land of the Pueblo and taking of
these lands will have a disastrous effect
upon the subsistence economy of the
Pueblo members ..."

In exchange for suffering all these claimed damages,
the Cochiti reserved to themselves "... the right to
develop or lease for development said area for any
and all commercial purposes attendant to the operation of the reservoir. ..."

Faced with imminent development of a major recreational attraction completely beyond their own
experience, the Cochiti turned to their legally appointed guardian, the Bureau of Indian Affairs, for
advice on how best to take advantage of the opportunity that had been thrust upon them. The BIA's

reflex response was to commission a study. In 160 pages, the consultants' report quantified the obvious: a recreational development at Cochiti Lake would attract "over three-quarters of a million man-days use." (Among the customers, presumably, would be the 2,600 people who already owned boats in bone-dry Albuquerque.) According to the Corps of Engineers' cost-benefit figures—used, and often manipulated, to prove the economic value of a project— one day's boating at Cochiti Lake would be "worth" $2, and one day's fishing would represent 50 cents in "benefit." (Presumably, then, one day's fishing from one boat would add up to a $2.50 "benefit" to someone.)

Whatever type of development was selected, the report admitted, the effect on Cochiti culture and life would be traumatic. "The impact . . . of Cochiti Dam and the consequent influx of people into the area has yet to be felt by the average Cochiti. . . . It is difficult to assess, or even visualize, the changes which will affect every Cochiti. A people who have adhered to their time-honored way of life will see the faster tempo right at their doorstep. Each Cochiti will find himself re-evaluating his position, and will be seeking ways to adjust even his daily life to a rapidly changing daily scene."

Thus forewarned, the Bureau of Indian Affairs brokered a marriage between the Cochiti tribe and the California Cities Development Company to create the City of Cochiti Lake. As the BIA must have known, but the Cochiti evidently did not, even in the demimonde of desert subdividers California Cities was notorious for land-hustling. If the suburbanization of the Cochiti reservation was the preferred means of improving the Indians' economic and social lot—itself a debatable conclusion—the selection of California Cities as the partner most likely to benefit the Cochiti or to ease their transition into the modern world was even more questionable.

California Cities, which sold out to Great Western United on the eve of signing the lease for Cochiti Lake, was the creation of the fabled "Desert Baron," M. Penn Phillips. Long before California Cities, Phillips was credited with some of the most inventive ruses for selling desert acreage to greedy suckers. One classic involved erecting a dummy oil-well derrick near the sales office. Salesmen were instructed studiously to avoid questions about the unavoidable curiosity, thus insuring that the potential buyer would jump to the conclusion that he was buying into a bonanza.

By the time the Bureau of Indian Affairs was looking around for someone to guide the Cochiti into the world of commerce, Phillips and his younger partner, Nathan K. Mendelsohn, were picking up the last few marbles at another desert subdivision, their biggest yet, the 80,000-acre California City. Remotely situated in the American Sahara southeast of Mojave, California, the subdivision was for all practical purposes as uninhabitable as the moon. Phillips and Mendelsohn were able to buy up the land for a reported average price of $37 an acre. According to *The New Mexico Review,* a 25,000-acre parcel owned by the state of California was transferred to the developers for a total price of $10. Using the sales and marketing methods learned in Phillips' half-century of subdividing in California, the two promoters were able to sell the land for $10,000 to $20,000 an acre.

Prospective buyers were taken by simple gimmicks. The infernal desert summers and arctic winters were averaged in the promotional literature to a balmy 75 degrees. An abundance of underground water was demonstrated by a recirculating artificial pond, complete with waterfall and lined with plastic to keep the water from seeping away. Rampant development was indicated by a cluster of model-home shells, mostly unsold; idle industrial facilities; and a group of tenantless town houses.

Nevertheless, by 1968, after 10 years of successful high-pressure lot selling, California City had fewer than 1,200 permanent residents. In 1968 and 1969, more than six hundred property owners at California City finally got wise and sued Mendelsohn, Phillips and their corporations for fraud, deceit and misrepresentation.

In the meantime, however, California Cities had entered into partnership with the Cochiti Indians for the development of Cochiti Lake. And almost simultaneously, California Cities sold its business—California City, a newer subdivision called Colorado City, and the proposed Cochiti project—to the Great Western United conglomerate, purveyors of sugar beets, fast-food pizza franchises, and now, new towns on Indian land. For Great Western, the acquisition was a simple matter of numbers: California Cities' 1968 sales of more than $30 million and profits of over $7 million looked good on the balance sheet. Indeed, William White, the young venture capitalist behind Great Western, brought Nathan K. Mendel-

sohn onto the board of directors of Great Western
to direct the Cochiti Lake operation. Mendelsohn
was the only person at Great Western with credentials of any kind in the land-development business.
Evidently, he was able to convince at least some of
the Cochiti to trust him. After a junket to California
City and Colorado City, the tribal council dubbed
their new master builder "Moo-Kathra"—The Lion.

Mendelsohn's sales force went to work in the old,
accustomed ways. Before there was a drop of water
in the lake—indeed, before the dam was fairly begun
—billboards announcing the ultimate city, the "seven
day weekend," lined the interstate between Albuquerque and Santa Fe. Full-page ads appeared
throughout the state. Lots were hustled as investments that would double in value once Cochiti Lake
was a reality.

In return for the permanent alteration of their ancestral land, the 400 Cochitis will receive a guaranteed income of $5 million over 99 years, plus a small
annual rental from each of Great Western's sub-
lessees, plus unspecified access to whatever jobs the
subdivision generates. The lot buyers will get subleases until April 30, 2068, at which time the Cochitis
regain their land with all improvements. In the interim, the sublessee can either live on his property
when and if development takes place or hold it for
resale in the hope that its market value will increase.
Meanwhile, the desert between Albuquerque and
Santa Fe has been carved up and resculpted by yet
another subdivision, and a lake to boot, subsidized
and promoted by the federal government at the taxpayers' expense.

Fred Cordero, Cochiti tribal council chairman during the negotiations with the Corps of Engineers, expressed the Indians' ambivalence about the inevitable. "We shall continue to grow our crops," he promised, "to have our sacred ceremonials. Children will no doubt still splash and swim in the acequias. For a time it will seem that little has changed. But gradually changes will come. Those of my age and generation have seen many of them and these will doubtless come faster and faster. Today we take a great step forward into an experience that is new and strange to us."

By 1970, however, the Cochiti had a better idea of what they had been backed into. Fifty-seven million cubic yards of earth from the Cochiti's sacred ancestral homeland were being moved into the path of the Rio Grande. Great Western's planners were dividing up the seamless desert into tiny lots, while Great Western's salesmen were huckstering the Indians' land and culture to white people anxious to invest in a natural world they had abandoned and a tradition that belonged to someone else. The Cochitis' growing unease was expressed by Sam Arquero to the pueblo in the language of diplomacy that is the white man's legacy to the Indian: "No one person can take the credit, the blame, or the responsibility for all that is taking place on our homeland."

By the time the New Mexico legislature was trying to decide whether Indian lands should—or could—be included in any 1972 subdivision control act, development at Cochiti was well under way. The dam was rising, and lot sales were booming. The legislators' attention was focused on another pueblo subdivision, Colonias de Santa Fe, on the Tesuque reservation north of the capital. There, the Sangre de Cristo Development Company, named for the mountains on the horizon, had struck a deal with the Indians almost identical to the arrangement between the Cochiti and Great Western. Indeed, the two contracts had been negotiated for the Indians by the same consultant, called in by the Department of the Interior "late in the game, to turn a lousy contract into a better one." And the same Albuquerque consulting firm did the land-use survey.

Sangre de Cristo was understandably anxious to protect its status as a partner of the Tesuque. Its 99-year lease with the tribe saved the company the expense of assembling the acreage and buying it outright. And the exemption of Indian lands from local, state and federal laws, designed to insure Indian independence on the little land left to them, was seized by Sangre de Cristo as license to ignore subdivision regulations in Santa Fe County. Under the protection of the Tesuques, the company planned one-third-acre lots, instead of the one-acre minimum required by the county, thereby tripling the concentration of septic tanks and wells. The county would be powerless to require proof that water was available. Theoretically, the subdivision might even be exempt from state liquor and gambling laws (the Sandia Pueblo, near Albuquerque, had already been proposed as a site for a race track) and property and sales taxes would not apply.

As its representative in Santa Fe Sangre de Cristo had one of its incorporators, none other than Fred

Standley, ex-state attorney general and former campaign director for U.S. Senator Joseph M. Montoya. In the pattern of chronic incest that mixes politics and land in New Mexico, Sangre de Cristo had other friends in high places.

The same law firm whose partner fought Sangre de Cristo's subdivision battles also boasted former New Mexico governor Jack Campbell on its roster with "of counsel" status. Campbell became the counsel for the Tesuque Pueblo, later resigning the job to the accompaniment of criticism in the Santa Fe press. Before Campbell's law firm got involved with Sangre de Cristo another partner, Donnan Stephenson, was elected to the New Mexico Supreme Court, which referees questions involving the interests of both Sangre de Cristo and the Tesuque Pueblo.

Such consanguinity in the ruling class is nothing unusual, of course, nor does it necessarily indicate any impropriety to compare with the clear conflicts of interest elsewhere in the New Mexico mixture of land and politics. Nevertheless, such professional and friendly alliances might well add to the existing skepticism about the atmosphere in which important subdivision decisions are made in Santa Fe.

The coalition of developers, ranchers and others opposed to meaningful subdivision regulation in the Thirtieth Session took every occasion to promote legislation and amendments that would exempt the Indian pueblos from coverage under any law that might pass. The legislative battle created ironic alliances. Siding with the pro-subdivision interests were various Indian representatives, who sincerely felt that development—even with the lion's share of the

profits leaving the reservations—was the best thing
for their tribesmen. Among the forces fighting for
strong subdivision regulation were other Indians who
claimed—as the traditional Hopis have claimed in
Arizona—that the tribal councils were creatures of
the BIA, and had acquiesced in a bargain-basement
sale of valuable Indian rights without consulting the
majority of the tribe. Some Indians also insisted that
the developments proposed for their reservations
would violate sacred ground and overpower traditional ways, and ought to be refused at any price.
The strength of Sangre de Cristo and its allies con-
gregated in Santa Fe was sufficient to have the subject of Indian lands excluded from the proposed bill
even before the legislation was cynically compromised and mercifully killed.

Meanwhile, the collaboration between Sangre de
Cristo and the Tesuque had inspired at least three
legal actions. One, filed by New Mexico's attorney
general, David Norvell, seeks to establish that Indian
lands under lease to non-Indian entrepreneurs are
subject to state jurisdiction. The case is important
as a test for similar situations that are already arising
with other pueblos: a Great Western claim of im-
munity from state regulation at Cochiti was settled
out of court when Great Western backed down. In
practical terms, however, even a reassertion by
the courts of state jurisdiction will have little effect
until meaningful state subdivision regulations are
enacted. The litigation does not seek to affirm the
jurisdiction of Santa Fe County, whose regulations
are the only ones Colonias de Santa Fe is flouting.
And even if they were ratified by the courts, the

county regulations might in the end prove as flexible for Colonias de Santa Fe as they did for AMREP's Eldorado.

A second suit was filed by a coalition of environmentalists and Harvey Mudd's Central Clearing House, charging that the marriage between the Sangre de Cristo Development Company and the Tesuque tribe should be annulled because the matchmaker, the BIA's parent Department of the Interior, had failed to file an environmental impact statement as required by the National Environmental Policy Act. In November 1972, a federal appeals court in Denver ruled that the Bureau of Indian Affairs had violated the law in approving the subdivision without a thorough study of its effects on the environment.

The third suit was filed by the Native American Legal Defense and Education Fund, a foundation-sponsored agency, in the name of some 50 Tesuques acting on behalf of the tribe. Their complaint charged that the Bureau of Indian Affairs and the Sangre de Cristo Development Company were partners in a fraud perpetrated against the Tesuques. According to the complaint, the tribe's income from the lease will be under one dollar per year for each acre, $99 for the term of the lease, while the subdividers plan to sublease the land for as much as $27,000 per acre. Moreover, the suit alleges that the Tesuque water rights transferred to the developer will preclude irrigation essential to the tribe's agriculture, while the subdivision's close-packed septic tanks will pollute the pueblo's underground domestic water supply. Not least in a long list of complaints is the allegation that the terms of the lease were never fully explained to the tribal council, much less to the tribe at large, either by the developer or by the Indians' own guardian, the BIA.

At this writing, two of the cases are still in court, and it may be years before the basic issues involved are finally decided. Meanwhile, the Bureau of Indian Affairs has announced no change in its policy of delivering the Indians into the waiting hands of subdividers willing to develop their lands. And, as the Chamber of Commerce folks like to tell tourists in search of something exotic but handy, there are 19 pueblos strung out along the Rio Grande. Each is as suitable for subdivision as Cochiti or Tesuque.

9.
California:
Getting it
all together

If subdivisions flourish in the inhospitable South-western desert, they grow rampant in California's fertile culture medium. In part, the success of the subdividers in California is due to the social and cultural climate of the state, a hothouse atmosphere in which people's dreams and the schemes that cater to them take on fantastic forms and proportions. California, as has been remarked before, is not so much a state as a state of mind. What America has been to generations of restless Europeans, California is to Americans: the New World, the place where anything is always possible, where a person can make a new start, get a second chance. That California, spiritually as well as geographically, represents the last chance, the dead end of the American westward odyssey, only lends an air of urgency to the quest.

Hardly any social or cultural innovation—retread ideology or religion, scheme for self-improvement or personal salvation—no matter how outrageous to reason or health, fails to find its adherents in California.

For companies catering to dreams of success, security and the good life with half-acre lots in remote subdivisions, the California gold rush is never-ending. Since 1963, the state of California has protected its home-grown subdividers from the rigors of out-of-state competition by requiring non-California promoters to register their land offerings as securities, subject to the same stringent regulation as stock or bond issues.

This means, for one thing, that in order to sell his lots in California, an out-of-state subdivider has to post bond for the completion of all improvements he promises to his customers. If he describes the wonders of things to come—paved roads, utilities, recreational facilities, schools, or whatever—he has to satisfy the state that he is good for the cost. This is a major roadblock to operators intending to tie up as little capital as possible in actual improvements, and to finance any eventual development with the receipts from lot sales.

Even more devastating to the ambitions of outsiders anxious to operate in the California market, the state's securities law insists that the price of any offering be demonstrably "fair, just and equitable." In terms of unimproved lots in promotional subdivisions, this means that the price must bear some relationship to the price of comparable land in surrounding areas. Any such formula would disallow not only the exorbitant profits on subdivision lots, one-third of the sales price by the industry's own rule of thumb, but also much of the other third commonly earmarked for promotion and sales expenses.

According to a complaint filed by the California attorney general's office on September 21, 1971, GAC's Rio Rico operation in Arizona has tried to circumvent the California securities law by "luring California residents . . . to Las Vegas, Nevada, . . . by promising such enticements as free drinks, free dinners, free hotel rooms and free shows in Las Vegas." For the most part, however, the application of securities law to real-estate offerings has effectively discouraged the interstate land-sales industry from selling in California. Yet the virtual elimination of out-of-state competition has left the California market wide open to the burgeoning numbers of home-grown promoters, who are not affected by the securities law. Operating under the far less stringent state real-estate regulations for intrastate subdivisions, native entrepreneurs are free to peddle California lots in state and out. The result has been a frenzy of activity: some half million acres registered for subdivision between 1960 and 1970, and 561 California projects registered with HUD for interstate sale.

The prime sites for California subdividers are located along the coastline, where land prices had been driven as high as $4,000 per front-foot by the time a 1972 law limited new coastal development. In any event, by 1972 there wasn't much coastline left to develop. More than two-thirds of California's 1,072-mile coastline is already sequestered in private hands, while another 55 miles of the public portion are reserved for the exclusive use of the military.

More than a dozen miles of the most spectacular northern California coastline were lost to one conspicuously elegant subdivision called Sea Ranch. In the 1960's, national magazines celebrating the sexy, trendy lifestyles germinating in California seldom failed to include a spread on Sea Ranch in glorious sunset color. The project's core area was developed in a style of rustic sophistication which took every award for architectural and design excellence. Raw board siding pickled gray-brown in the briny Pacific breeze, and steep shed roofs echoed the colors and contours of the hilly site. There were plenty of eye-catching angles, interior spaces on multiple levels and windows aimed at the setting sun or particular landscape *tableaux*. The site plan for the first thousand acres clustered the buildings in the shelter of existing hedgerows, leaving almost all of the land in grassy fields and woods sloping to the sea. According to Lawrence Halprin & Associates, the celebrated San Francisco planning firm that did the original design for the first part of Sea Ranch, "It was a very strong, ecologically based plan . . . to preserve the character of the land."

A professional citation to Halprin is still prominently displayed in the Sea Ranch sales office, but that is the only continuing influence he maintains over the development. In fact, the Halprin firm is no longer associated with Sea Ranch, and Halprin himself has complained publicly about the perversion of his land-use plan. Although his original architecture still sets the style for subsequent building, the vital cluster plan has been abandoned in favor of a traditional one-lot-one-house subdivision scheme.

The site will eventually be cluttered with houses on individual small lots, but Sea Ranch's developer, Oceanic Properties, a subsidiary of Castle & Cooke, sells the subdivision as a private nature preserve. Visitors are given a brochure titled "Whales and Wild Iris: A Guide to The Sea Ranch," listing local "flora and fauna to observe and study." (No illustrations are provided, however, to help the nature-lover distinguish between the Yellow Lupine and the Blue, or among Cat's Ear, Cow Parsnip and Monkey Flower.) "Great white beaches and coves to explore," describe the Sea Ranch ads. On "the loveliest stretch of unspoiled north coast . . . every Sea Ranch resident will have free and equal access to the shore."

Along miles of "the loveliest stretch of unspoiled north coast," then, Sea Ranch residents are more free and equal than the rest of the population, which is barred from the beach altogether. "You'll find relief here from the daily crush of people," promise the ads. "The Sea Ranch is a private development, for the exclusive use of Sea Ranch residents and their guests. Access is guarded by a full-time security patrol."

Sea Ranch's arrogation of the shoreline seems, however, to violate the explicit provisions and spirit of the California Constitution, Article XV, Section 2, titled *"People Shall Always Have Access to Navigable Waters"*:

> No individual, partnership, or corporation claiming or possessing the frontage or tidal lands of a harbor, bay, inlet, estuary, or other navigable water in this State, shall be

permitted to exclude the right of way to such water whenever it is required for any public purpose, nor to destroy or obstruct free navigation of such water . . .

Moreover, to define the intention of such troublesome phrases as "right of way" and "free access" and "public purpose," the authors of the constitution added at the end of Section 2:

. . . the Legislature shall enact such laws as will give the most liberal construction to this provision, so that access to the navigable waters of this State shall be always attainable for the people thereof.

Despite the clear instructions of the constitution, the California legislature had passed no laws to implement Article XV, Section 2, by the time Oceanic Properties bought the Sea Ranch property, about eight square miles, in 1964. The original development permit, covering the first third of the plan, was issued by the county with provision for "designated area or areas for the purpose of public access to the ocean. . . ." No such access was provided.

When the plan for the remainder of Sea Ranch was announced, it provided only some 100 acres at the extreme end of the property, less than 2 percent of the total land, for a public park. The rest of the unbroken coastline would be exclusively for Sea Ranchers. Although the plan was accepted by the Sonoma County Planning Board, within two months of the approval 1,400 letters were filed in opposition. When the county supervisors ignored this protest, anti-Sea Ranch citizens formed a group called Citizens Organized to Acquire Access to State Tidelands

(COAAST). The group sought to force a referendum to insure "public access corridors to publicly owned tidelands" to be spaced no more than one mile apart. After the supervisors rejected their petition, COAAST went to court and won a place on the ballot as Proposition B.

Oceanic Properties mounted a strong and expensive campaign against this threat to its sovereignty over the California coast. Its budget was estimated at $50,000, against less than $2,500 spent by COAAST. There were newspaper ads—and editorials—against Proposition B on any number of irrelevant or specious grounds: that the access would cost tax money, that there was nothing down there worth having access to, and so on. As November drew near, the issue was blitzed by the developer's campaign. Proposition B lost the vote by a 10 percent margin, and along the miles of Sea Ranch's stylish elite coastal subdivision, except for the "park" at one end, the public still has no access to the Pacific.

Sea Ranch takes some pains with its land in order to attract sophisticated tenants. Its customers are pleased to pay high prices for exclusive enjoyment of an environment that is, in part, arguably in the public domain. Farther north, in Humboldt County, "where the Pacific meets the Redwood country," the developers of Shelter Cove have been far less solicitous of the landscape and their clientele. The name of the development may inspire visions of a snug harbor for visiting boats, but Shelter Cove is located on a chronically fogbound, storm-lashed promontory south of Cape Mendocino, astride the San Andreas Fault. The only land access is over a *grand prix* road, winding for 23 miles from Highway 101 near Garberville.

Remote from population centers, steeply sloped and vulnerable to severe weather and earthquakes, Shelter Cove is a perfect example of an inappropriate site for intensive subdivision. Nevertheless, its developers carved the 2,640-acre former sheep ranch into 4,780 lots, some smaller than one-eighth of an acre, and priced each at $6,000 minimum—the equivalent of $50,000-plus per acre. At those rates, the development made back its land cost of $780,000 on the first 15 acres sold. The sales campaign was nationwide, including Hawaii. California customers were treated to free plane trips to the site, free meals and drinks. At Shelter Cove, the unimproved land was festooned with signs proclaiming the wonders to come. "Please pardon the inconvenience," said one sign farther back in the hills. "This road is being improved and realigned to Shelter Cove," though no roadwork had been done or even contracted for. "PLANNED SITE MEANDERING BOARD-WALK" read another sign. The lots, many of them so steep as to defy architectural ingenuity, others leveled with loose earth fill up to 60 feet deep on the hillsides, sold like beer in Bavaria.

There were things about Shelter Cove that lot buyers were not told. For one, the "free access to the beaches" promised by the developer to "all residents of Shelter Cove" was in fact contingent on a leased right-of-way which could not be guaranteed. More important, the "improvements" that gave the appearance of development to the property to stimulate sales—the roads, sewers, water and power systems—were financed by a bonded debt of $5.4 million which was passed along to the lot buyers, who were in the embarrassing position of paying for the same things twice. The bonds were secured by liens on the lot owners' property. In time, the lot owners would be liable for further assessments to pay for future improvements.

If the customers were mistreated at Shelter Cove, the land was sorely manhandled. The error of bull-dozing roads and terracing hillsides in such climate and terrain as Shelter Cove's became obvious early in the game. In the winter of 1965-66, the area was hit by a big rainstorm, no more severe than many that had attacked the coast time and time again through-out the land's long history. This time, however, the water runoff was not slowed by vegetation on the steep slopes. Instead, it coursed down 44 miles of paved roads, flooded storm sewers, flowed over de-nuded hillsides. Shelter Cove turned to mud and began to ooze downhill toward the ocean. Before it was over, 43 lots had been completely washed out, and damage was estimated at $1 million on a tract of land that had sold *in toto* not long before for $780,000. By early 1970, with very few houses in place on the five-year-old subdivision, the county supervisors estimated that it would take as much as $2 million to repair the roads. The grand jury has since warned the county against accepting respon-sibility for maintaining the roads.

Shelter Cove and Sea Ranch are not simply iso-lated insults to the celebrated wonders of the north-ern California coast. For their 1971 study, *Power and Land in California*, members of Ralph Nader's study group surveyed an arbitrarily selected 50-mile stretch of the shore north of San Francisco, starting in northern Marin County and continuing through most of Sonoma. Beginning at Marin's Dillon Beach, they found only 21.25 of the 50 miles of shore undeveloped. All but one of the developments had been established since 1965. Twelve additional miles of shoreline were planned for sale to developers, ultimately leaving only 12-and-a-fraction of the 50 miles the way the wind and the sea made them.

Inland, California is hardly in better shape, from the Oregon border all the way to Mexico. The half-million rural acres subdivided in the 1960's alone are enough to accommodate three million boondockers, assuming a generous half-acre average per lot, and a modest three people per house. And many more homesites—perhaps as many as were created by out-and-out subdividing—were added by "lot splitting" and "quartering," legal devices which permit small projects to become de facto subdivisions in spite of local planning and zoning regulations. Even without tenants, the California Division of Soil Conservation charges, the initial preparation of the land has resulted in "water pollution, loss of fish and wildlife habitat, damage to watercourses, lakes, and reservoirs, impairment of recreational opportunities, and sediment and flood damage to property."

According to the Nader group's report, Siskiyou County was the site of more than 70 subdivisions in less than 10 years, despite the fact that the county's growth rate is a leisurely 240 people per year. Sierra County, with a population of 2,500 people, has several subdivisions with room for 25,000 people each. One subdivision platted in Shasta County would house that county's entire population. All this pell-mell land-fractioning and environmental destruction have resulted in precious little actual development. In Madera County, the Nader study group found that over a period of 20 years, only 100 houses had been built on 21,048 subdivided lots. In general, the study found a construction rate of 1 percent or less per year on subdivision lots in heavily subdivided counties. Clearly, the environment is not being sacrificed to provide homes for people.

The case of Nevada County, one of the hardest-hit by the subdividers, is typical of the trend toward inappropriate subdivision. Nevada is a large, rural county extending from an altitude of 1,000 feet above sea level in the Sierra Nevada foothills to 7,000 feet in the mountains. Bypassed by immigration since the Gold Rush days, the county in 1965 had a population of only 25,100. The most optimistic projections envisioned a growth to 45,000 by 1980, but the State Department of Finance estimated only 28,000. By 1970, the population had increased by only 1,400 people, to 26,500, so the more conservative projection seems justified. Nevertheless, Nevada County has 50,000 subdivided acres. And according to Harold Berliner, district attorney of the county until 1973, "If the next five years show the same rate of increase in lots the last five years have shown (about 225 percent per year), *by the end of 1974 every square inch of privately held land in Nevada County will have been subdivided into suburban-style lots.*" Berliner's apocalyptic forecast seems justified: in the first three months of 1970 alone, plans were approved or proposed for 14,491 superfluous homesites.

Berliner also notes that "the strange thing about it all is that while lots increase like rabbits, the building rate—an average of 233 houses per year in the entire county—remains nearly constant. In the past six years, Nevada County authorized 8,510 'recreational' subdivision lots, on only 159 of which houses were built and placed on the tax rolls."

In 1970, California's Environmental Quality Study Council paid special attention to Nevada County. Among the items in its "memorandum of facts":

- At Lake of the Pines in Nevada County the developer [Boise Cascade] bought land at $873.30 per acre and sold it one year later for from $12,000 to $36,000 per acre.
- Serious degradation to the natural land and water environment will occur, including direct impacts upon public health, wildlife, and alternate land uses.
- An estimated 160 miles of streams (37 percent of the stream mileage within Nevada County) have already been damaged by siltation, stream-bank alterations and domestic waste discharges resulting from subdivision development.
- Much of the land occupied by subdivisions within Nevada County is located in the pine-chaparral or woodland-chaparral habitat zones, both of which are particularly important to deer and upland game species. Hunting opportunities have al-

ready been sharply curtailed on much of this land and the value of the land for wildlife is expected to diminish steadily as more homes are constructed. Some of the land now being subdivided is deer winter range which is already in critically short supply.

- Poorly designed subdivision roads are one of the biggest sources of silt pollution in Nevada County. For example, eroding road fills within a recent subdivision have discharged so much sediment . . . that salmon spawning gravels in the Yuba River will be severely damaged if the erosion is not arrested. The Yuba River salmon fishery is worth about $600,000 annually.

The 50,000 or more spoiled acres in Nevada County are by no means unusual. Indeed, they are dwarfed by the 100,000 acres of a single development, California City, in Kern County. California City, the state's third largest city in area, is "probably the largest desert land promotion ever offered," according to the attorney general of California. It is the most ambitious project of that group of investors, headed by Nathan K. Mendelsohn and M. Penn Phillips, which later sold it, along with Cochiti Lake, to Great Western United.

In 1969, California City achieved the special distinction of being the subject of an official investigative report by the California attorney general's office. The investigation was paid for by the taxpayers of California, but the resulting report was evidently suppressed until it was obtained and published by the Nader study group.

The lengthy state report constitutes a point-by-point indictment that might be applied in at least some of its particulars to almost any inappropriate rural subdivision. Among the allegations against California City by the attorney general's investigators:

- The developer has transformed uneconomic farmland acquired at $109 an acre into a "planned city" with lots that the development company sells for $9,000. Lots being sold today are without utilities or water or any paved road linking them to a one-block group of stores located 10 to 20 miles away. . . . To date, the developer has sold 32,000 parcels at a total sales price of $102 million to purchasers throughout the U.S., Germany and the Philippines.

- Although the developer has attempted to attract industry and provides recreational and community facilities (using over $6 million in public financing) there is no significant industrial development and the population of 896 is almost entirely dependent on the developer for employment or income.

- To prospective land buyers, California City is represented as a safe, secure real estate investment in a community with "abundant water." These representations are false. Purchasers desiring to sell find no ready market of buyers. Instead, when they are fortunate enough to resell they usually take a loss.

- His is no ordinary real estate sales scheme

—Mendelsohn isn't trying to sell 'land' and
the public isn't really buying the 'land.'
They are engaged in a grand illusion of
creating wealth. Mendelsohn has a dream
and the buyers believe the developer's
dream is capable of providing them with a
pot of gold. The art of creating gold from
base metals has long eluded our grasp, but
N. K. Mendelsohn has perfected the art of
turning desert dust into gold—but only for
himself. . . .

The report notes that political control of California
City is firmly in the hands of the developer, not the
land-owning citizens.

When California City became incorporated
in December 1965 . . . control of local affairs
passed into the hands of individuals favor-
ably oriented toward the needs of the
developer. Several employees of the developer who reside in California City are active in city and district affairs. An employee
of the developer has served as a member of
the city council since the incorporation of
the city and is presently Mayor. . . . A recent
survey of employees in the area indicates
that of the 238 residents now employed, 141
either work for the developer or are employed in the nineteen local businesses
heavily dependent on the developer's promotional activities. . . .

The attorney general's investigators further noted
that after "twelve years of its development, California City . . . is mainly inhabited by cactus, snakes,

and employees of the developer." The report quotes an editorial from the March 19, 1964, *California City Chronicle*, evidently written by some poorer-but-wiser property owner:

> Residents of California City are troubled by the absence of a medical center, the rutted, washboard roads, and the absence of a sewer system. To the residents, these improvements are priority items, but the developer, who resides in Santa Monica, proposed to build a 'million dollar city hall' instead.
>
> When citizens question the developer's actions he publicly labels them as 'cynics' and 'Doubting Thomases' with 'scornful' and 'negative' attitudes.
>
> Nevertheless, because of the developer's subsidization of the community and his dominant influence in community affairs, for the foreseeable future the desires of the developer will receive priority over the needs of the community.

The attorney general's investigators surveyed California City "investors" to learn what specific assurances they had received from the developer or his representatives regarding the availability of services, amenities and opportunities at the project.

> Fifty-three percent had been informed there was an underground lake capable of meeting future water needs; 61 percent had been informed that Feather River water would be available . . . ; 44 percent of the investors had been informed that major in-

dustries have purchased land in California City; 43 percent had been informed that major businesses have purchased sites in California City; 61 percent had been informed there was an international airport . . . adjacent to California City; and 23 percent had been informed a state college will be built in California City.

Needless to say, few, if any, of these persuasive claims had the slightest chance of coming true. By the same token, it is not surprising that the investment value of California City lots was less secure than the developer's salesmen were wont to promise. The attorney general's investigators analyzed all resales of California City lots from March 1968 to March 1969 in the two most developed tracts, i.e., those presumably having the highest resale value. Of the 20 such transactions, only four resulted in an apparent profit to the seller. The average loss on each of the other lots was $295.01. This analysis does not include lots that were for sale but failed to attract a buyer at any price. Nor does it consider the loss of potential earnings on money tied up in California City land instead of in other investments. For instance, one lucky seller, who bought Lot 272 in Tract 2066 at California City in 1958 for $990, sold it in 1968 for $2,000. After deductions for interest and taxes, his apparent profit was $647.42. Assuming that he put 10 percent down in 1958 and paid off the balance over the 10 years until he sold it, his average investment in the land throughout the period was $544.50. His average payments for interest and taxes came to $181.29 more. The total—

$725.79—banked at 6 percent compounded for 10 years would have grown to $1,299.15, or a profit of $573.36. His high-risk investment came out $74.06 ahead of the bank, or less than $7.50 a year. The majority of sellers, who had apparent losses, would have had to make comparable adjustments to their out-of-pocket deficits to take the true measure of their defeats.

The state of California has never released the attorney general's report to the public that paid for it; nor did the state go to court, as the report recommended, in support of a rash of legal actions by late-awakening California City landowners. Had the report been made public, with its catalogue of tricks and strategems in their most blatant manifestations, perhaps the public would have been better armed against the promotions of less flagrant operators. By the same token, subdivision promoters might have taken warning from a vigorous prosecution by the state in the California City case, and reformed their own questionable practices. And other, legitimate companies might have been spared costly experiments in the subdivision business.

10.
California:
Boise's cascade

On June 10, 1972, a sunny Saturday, the Lake of the Pines subdivision in the Sierra Nevada foothills of California held its "Independence Day" celebration. The pre-lunch-to-after-dusk festivity marked the transfer of the subdivision's facilities from the developer, Boise Cascade Recreation Communities Group, to the Lake of the Pines Property Owners Association. The association directors, elected by the few lot owners actually in residence, would henceforth be responsible for the maintenance, operation and administration of what the enthusiastic local newspaper catalogued as "a 230-acre lake, 18-hole golf course, clubhouse, pro shop, swimming pool, marina, beaches, playground, parks and tennis courts." They would collect and disburse membership dues, pegged between $50 and $180 per year, from the owners of each of the 1,937 lots in Lake of the Pines' 1,320 acres, only five percent of whom had built homes in the subdivision.

The modest bar in the clubhouse overlooking the man-made lake was doing a festive business. No one seemed to notice that the development's showpiece building was already overcrowded with even fewer people than it might expect regularly once Lake of the Pines was completely built, whenever—if ever— that happened. Boise was represented by Robert E. Yoxall, its director of recreation facilities, whose modish hairstyle and suit, not to mention his relative youth, made him conspicuous among the older, middle-American residents from Lake of the Pines. There were speeches before the buffet lunch. The clubhouse was decorated with flags, bunting and committee-made signs proclaiming "Independence Day." On each table was a plastic pot containing a live pine seedling to be transplanted to each owner's lot, and a tiny American flag. Before the golf tournament and other activities of the day began, Boise Cascade and the Lake of the Pines association joined in planting a blue spruce in front of the clubhouse, "as testimonial," enthused the local newspaper, "to the continued growth of the recreational-residential development." As a fitting finale, the newspaper recorded, "Boise Cascade sponsored a traditional fireworks display over the lake at dusk for the large crowd of dinner-dance revelers."

The retrograde pace of actual building at Lake of the Pines might have suggested that the celebration was premature. Still, it must have come as something of a surprise to the people who had bought land from Boise, at Lake of the Pines or at the conglomerate's many other subdivisions in California and across the country, to learn barely a month later that Boise Cascade was backing out of the subdivision business. Certainly the financial community and Boise's shareholders were shocked: the setback cost the company more than $200 million, and led to a paper loss of almost $2 *billion* by its stockholders. It was one of the largest corporate fiascos in recent business history; according to *The Wall Street Journal*, Boise's write-off was four times as large as Ford's after the Edsel. By mid-October, Boise Cascade's guiding genius, Robert V. Hansberger, 52, felt obliged to resign as the company's chairman, chief executive officer and director.

For both Boise and its chief, the sudden collapse had been preceded by a heady rise. Starting in 1957 with a single lumber company, Hansberger began to add to Boise with a dizzying series of 33 mergers and acquisitions. After buying more lumber companies, Boise was strong enough to expand into related fields: timberland, pulp and paper, packaging; and finally into factory-built housing, on-site housing, and mobile homes, from which the move into land development must have seemed a logical step.

Sales, $35 million in 1957, topped $1 billion by 1968, a growth of 3,000 percent. Holders of what was obviously a hot stock were gratified by earnings that rose from 34 cents a share before Hansberger to $2.85 in 1969. Investors responded to the numbers by ballooning Boise's stock as high as $75 in 1969, from a starting point of $3 in 1957, adjusted for splits. Hansberger himself held some 200,000 shares, worth about $20 million at the top of the rise. Boise made the "*Fortune* 500" list of corporate stars and headed for the top, reaching the number 55 position in 1969 with sales of $1.726 billion, and net income of $84 million.

Success also earned for Bob Hansberger and Boise a *Fortune* profile, far more flattering than a simple listing among the 500. According to *Fortune* in October 1969, "Hansberger has put an intellectual stamp on his company. A star graduate in a celebrated class at Harvard Business School (1947), he has been a recruiter of M.B.A.'s and a believer in trying new tools of analysis and decision. He and his top executives make an annual three-day pilgrimage to Stanford where they submit to the scrutiny of M.B.A. candidates in seminars—as a result of which Boise Cascade, Hansberger believes, has become the subject of the largest case study ever done on any company."

Thus, Hansberger and his company basked in the admiration of the entire business world, and the successful conglomerator seemed only too willing to explain his recipe for getting it all together. The trick, he explained, was to expand in a coherent, integrated way, rather than simply picking up companies "because they're there." Noted *Fortune* approvingly, "He has made his acquisitions in accordance with a clearly defined pattern, whereas most conglomerators are uninhibited about acquiring a wide variety of unrelated industries." Hansberger's logic led him from lumber to pulp to paper to packaging, and so on, in what he called "congeneric" expansion. He wanted to make Boise Cascade "the General Motors of the industry," a vertically integrated giant.

The second secret, simply put, was to make money, lots of it, compounded year after year. His number-one objective, Hansberger told *Fortune* over and over again in the course of his interview, was "consistently to increase the earnings per share by 20 percent compounded annually," doubling them every three and one-half years. At the peak of his success in 1969, he still insisted, "We have a tough objective—20 percent compounded—and it keeps us lean and hungry each year. Our fellows are working harder than ever before. Our earnings per share were up 49 percent last year. So now this year we must try to go up 20 percent on a bigger base; thus the more we make, the tougher the job."

In view of Hansberger's guiding aims, the subdivision business was a likely exercise for Boise. Land subdivision seemed "tangibly related," in *Fortune's* phrase, to Boise's other activities. From its original lumber business, Boise was already knowledgeable about rural real estate. More important, housing in the new subdivisions could provide an additional market for Boise lumber, sold through Boise's own homebuilding division.

The subdivision business also promised to contribute mightily to Hansberger's goal of "an increase in earnings per share of 20 percent year after year." The huge profits possible in retail land sales—as high as 33 percent of sales—were only part of the benefits. By deferring development costs, and counting the entire amount of a land sale "on the downstroke"— when the contract was signed—Boise could give its apparent assets and earnings a healthy boost. At least for a while, as long as sales volume remained high.

So Boise moved into the land business, specializing in recreational subdivisions in California's Sierra Nevada foothills. As Hansberger confidently told the San Francisco Security Analysts Club as early as August 1963, "The Western frontier today is east of the West. It's in the country people have been flying over and driving through: between the Rockies and the Sierra Nevada and the Cascades."

In characteristic entrepreneurial style, Hansberger got Boise into the subdivision business mostly by acquisition—buying up other companies' projects. The real-estate section of the *San Francisco Chronicle* became a diary of Boise's activities. On April 4, 1968, for instance, the *Chronicle* reported that Boise had acquired the subdivisions of the R. A. Watts Co., Perma-Built Enterprises, U.S. Land Co., and Pacific Cascade Land Co. Just two weeks later, the paper noted Boise's purchase of 6,090 acres in the Rancho California development in Riverside County. Less than two months later, it was the 9,000 acres of the Crystal Bay Development Company at Incline Village on Lake Tahoe. In January 1969, Boise reached farther west to buy 25,000 acres of the Parker Ranch on the west coast of Hawaii's Big Island. Six months later, the company took an option on 7,000 acres at Horsehead Creek, near Three Rivers in Tulare County, and a year later another 1,580 acres was added at Lake Edison. When Boise's spree was over in 1972, it was lord of a scattered domain of 31 subdivisions: five clustered along the East Coast, seven in the Great Lakes region, 17 in California, and outposts in Hawaii and northern Washington state. In its hurry to get big, buying up existing companies right and left, Boise acquired liabilities as well as assets. Among the liabilities were salesmen steeped in the good old ways of doing business. Almost overnight, Boise became one of the biggest subdividers in the United States, and its sales operations were indistinguishable from the shoddy deceptions perpetrated by entrepreneurs who never made the pages of *Fortune* or the seminars at Stanford.

Boise Cascade also became adept at making powerful friends and influencing the right people. Boise wasn't the only one: influence of one kind or another is a fixture of the subdivision business in California, where cozy relationships between the real-estate industry and its regulators have been institutionalized.

At the top level, the Department of Real Estate in California is headed by a commissioner who, according to law, *must* have five years' experience as a real-estate broker—a member, in other words, of the very fraternity whose activities he is supposed to regulate. In practice, the commissioner is often an ex-president of the California Real Estate Association. Although the commissioner is required to surrender his broker's license before taking office, he is traditionally quick to renew it when he steps down. Most recently, for instance, commissioner Burton E. Smith left his government post in April 1971, to become senior vice president of a Beverly Hills realty and land-development firm. Smith's immediate predecessor in government was Milton C. Gordon, who soon became a consultant to California City. Further back, Dean D. Watson resigned as commissioner in 1957 to become an executive in the ranks of M. Penn Phillips.

In October 1971, journalist Lynn Ludlow of the *San Francisco Examiner* published the results of a three-year investigation of relationships between California public officials and land promoters. Among Ludlow's findings:

- Jess Unruh, former Speaker of the California Assembly, candidate for higher office, supporter of Robert Kennedy and Eugene McCarthy, went to work in 1971 as an "economic and ecological consultant" to Nathan K. Mendelsohn, purveyor of California City, Cochiti Lake and other projects.
- One of the former directors of California City was Frank Mankiewicz, a member of the Kennedy political fraternity and more recently a director of the McGovern campaign.
- San Francisco Mayor Joseph Alioto was a principal owner of a Nevada County subdivision, later sold to an outfit including among its owners a recent chairman of the California State Democratic Committee.
- Chief Deputy Attorney General Charles O'Brien accepted a $1,000 contribution and a $5,000 loan from real-estate promoter Jack Kirby during his unsuccessful 1970 campaign for attorney general. O'Brien also accepted a $5,000 contribution from Maurice "Mike" Inman, attorney for Shelter Cove and its sister subdivision to the south, Brooktrails.
- At Shelter Cove, the county planning director and the chairman of the Planning Commission were allowed to buy choice lots and sell them back to the developer at substantial profits.

• Last but not least on Ludlow's list of conflicts of interest, California Governor Ronald Reagan's son, who likes motorboats, had been employed as an "advisor" by the Tahoe-Donner subdivision in California, and Lake Havasu City in Arizona.

Boise's participation in government went considerably beyond its open-handed support of the electoral process. According to Ralph Nader's study group, "... one local D.A. was hired by Boise Cascade to handle a water problem in a neighboring county. A county planning director was hired off the public payroll by Boise Cascade midway through a development project. The mayor of a North Coast city is also Boise Cascade's public relations man for the area, while two of the five-man city council work for Boise Cascade and a third depends upon it for his business. In another area, the Boise Cascade task force patronized the hotel and restaurant of one of the County Supervisors, who also received free advertising in the company newspaper. In another county, the head of a project that had been purchased by Boise Cascade saw fit to take out a $40,000 life-insurance policy from an obscure midwestern company through its local agent, one of the County Supervisors, while another Supervisor was awarded a sizeable campaign contribution and yet another was graced by the project's purchase of three automobiles from his local dealership. . . . In another county, a member of the Planning Commission is a licensed Boise Cascade salesman. . . . Trips are a common ploy, and Boise Cascade made a plane available for one former County Supervisor running for statewide office."

Such wholehearted dedication made it possible for Boise to make rapid progress as a subdivider. By 1969 its recreation business, largely land sales, came to $209 million, about 12 percent of Boise's total. Along with Lake of the Pines, Lake Wildwood, Hidden Valley Lake, Pine Mountain Lake, Lake Don Pedro, not to mention Bar XX, Circle XX, Diamond XX and the rest of the California constellation, there were stellar attractions elsewhere in the country: Ocean Pines on the Maryland shore, Lake Tarleton in New Hampshire, Woodridge Lake in Connecticut, and others around the map.

Although Boise Cascade got into the subdivision business in a hurry, there was nothing slapdash about its projects. Boise was not in the business of selling vast desert wasteland, like California City. The typical Boise Cascade development was relatively small —a few thousand acres—and at least partially furnished with roads, water treatment plants, utilities, and other amenities. Chief among these were a golf course, with its attendant pro shop and clubhouse-restaurant, and an artificial lake behind an earthen dam. The golf course and the lake were the keys to the concept. Not only did they provide an alluring selling point for the entire development, they also created choice lots that could be sold for premium prices. An ordinary half-acre or less at a Boise development might go for $5,000-$7,000. Fronting on the lake, a similar-size lot would sell for $20,000 and up, and a "second-tier" lot just behind it or a lot on the golf course might bring $11,000-$15,000.

Still, such improvements involved substantial "front-end" expenses for the developer before the lot sales could begin, and certainly before the big payoff. Lake Wildwood was a more-or-less typical Boise operation: 2,300 acres of "core area" and another 1,060 for development later, with 3,445 lots in the core area and an eventual planned population of 4,500 families; 13 miles west of Grass Valley, California; with a 300-acre lake, and a par-72, 165-acre golf course; and all the rest. According to Boise's figures, its estimated development costs at Lake Wildwood were:

Land cost	$2,500,000
Engineering, consultants, permits, erosion control, landscaping	2,400,000
Dam and lake	2,000,000
Roads	3,100,000
Sewer system	3,100,000
Water system	3,300,000
Electrical system	100,000
Golf course	830,000
Playgrounds, parks, beaches	420,000
Clubhouse, pro shop	263,000
Beach club, pool	137,000
Campgrounds	150,000
Marina	67,000
Entrance, gate	64,000
Tennis courts	14,000
Equestrian facilities	15,000
TOTAL	$18,460,000

Even allowing for some exaggeration, this represents a large undertaking for any company to be repeating in development after development within the space of just a few years. As an index of how

Boise's front-end investment exceeded that of less open-handed subdividers, it is interesting to compare Lake Wildwood with, say, Rio Rancho Estates in New Mexico. For a community intended eventually for 4,500 residents, Boise claims it invested $16 million above the cost of the land: an average per-person investment of $3,555. Rio Rancho, on the other hand, projects 100,000 residents, but even after a decade of profitable operation can claim less than $20 million in front-end costs: an average investment of $200 per projected resident. In the standard glossy brochure that Boise adapted for each of its developments, the company boasted that all this care and expense was meant to attract "all kinds of people, from all kinds of places and all walks of life. . . . Residents only really have three things in common. They love to be outdoors, in the country, away from concrete and plastic. They love to play. And, in the immortal words of song, they love to love."

Sadly for Boise, which was halfway trying to build livable communities, "all kinds of people" were slow in relocating to its subdivisions. For all the buyers who actually turned their lot purchases into building plans, either for permanent residence or second-home use, Boise might just as well have been selling the Sahara Desert through the mail. A survey of all Lake of the Pines lot buyers by Nevada County D.A. Harold Berliner revealed that more than half had purchased their lots as speculative investments rather than as homesites. The fact that there was no foreseeable resale market for their lots only guaranteed that at least 50 percent of the lots in Boise's "communities" would remain vacant for a long time to come, their owners increasingly un-happy. A similar survey by Tuolumne County dis-trict attorney Ernest Geddes found that 249 of 351 respondents listed "investment and resale" as their chief reason for buying at Boise's Lake Don Pedro. There were indications that the same situation pre-vailed throughout Boise's empire. A researcher in 1972 found only 100 houses on Lake of the Pines' 1,944 lots; nine houses on 3,600 acres at Rancho Calaveras; one house each at the Diamond XX and Bar XX projects.

Taking the population of lot owners as a whole, future builders and would-be profiteers alike, it was a dissatisfied group, according to the Berliner survey at Lake of the Pines. To the question, *"If you could remake your decision to buy, based on knowl-edge acquired since you made that decision, would you have purchased your lot at the price you paid?"*, two-thirds of those replying said that they would not. More than half had their lots up for resale, but 85 percent expected less than a fair return on their in-vestment. Respondents complained of salesmen's broken promises, of disappointing recreational facili-ties and maintenance, high taxes and utility rates.

Customer complaints were only one of Boise's problems, as the company's intentions to subdivide across the country began to meet increased resist-ance from one local authority after another. In 1972, the Maryland Real Estate Commission halted sales at Boise's Ocean Pines development because some of the salesmen were operating without required li-censes. In New Hampshire, the state planning di-rector reported, "If we hadn't stepped in they would have been dumping that refuse from the 5,200-acre development into the lakes." The director of the Torrington, Connecticut, health district told a researcher, "I am endeavoring to get the real-estate commissioner to lift their license to sell, as the sewerage problem solution is very dim and far in the future, if at all. They, however, continue the big sales and TV push." Boise's move into a choice rural area near New York City was thwarted by aroused local forces.

There were troubles in California, too, some of them acquired unknowingly by Boise in its takeover binge. Costs at Lake of the Pines jumped $950,000 at a shot because D.A. Harold Berliner, the subdividers' nemesis, forced Boise's predecessor to install the water system that the developer had promised in its required public report but seemed never ready to build. At Lake Don Pedro, Boise was forced to import water from the next county for one part of the subdivision. To get water for the rest, Boise tried to trade 1,000 hastily acquired acres, soon to be flooded by a state-built lake, in return for water rights. Boise, of course, had made good use of the projected lake— part of a publicly funded $100-million water project —as the focal point of its subdivision, in order to boost the price of its land from $200 an acre to $7,000.

Worst of all for Boise was a series of three lawsuits. The first was brought in October 1971 in the name of the people of the state of California by California state attorney general Evelle J. Younger and William H. O'Malley, district attorney of the county of Contra Costa, against Boise Cascade Recreation Communities Corporation of Delaware, Boise Cas-

cade Home and Land Corporation, Boise Cascade
Credit Corporation, three Boise employees and executives, and 200 John Does "unknown to plaintiff."
A long list of illegitimate sales practices, described
in 31 legal-size pages, supported by 75 sworn dec-
larations, was alleged against Boise in the sale of
lots at four of its subdivisions in Calaveras County—
Rancho Calaveras, Bar XX, Diamond XX and Circle
XX. The suit charged that lots in Rancho Calaveras
had no investment value; that Boise had promised
recreational and other amenities which were not
available, or were available only at unadvertised
cost to the buyer; that assurances had been given
that major "freeways" would be located nearby, increasing the value of the development; that salesmen
used two-way radios "to deceive the prospective lot
purchasers . . . that lots are being sold rapidly; that
only a few lots are left for sale in the subdivision; and
that the purchaser must buy a lot immediately or the
one of his choice will be sold to someone else right
before his eyes."

In sum, the complaint asserted, "Defendants, and
each of them, knew or should have known with the
exercise of reasonable care about the making of
each one of the representations or omissions of fact
set forth . . . and knew or should have known with
the exercise of reasonable care that each and every
such representation or omission of fact was false and
misleading. . . . Defendants by scheme and design
conspired to deceive . . . members of the public. . . ."

The Superior Court of California for the County
of Contra Costa issued a preliminary injunction
against the defendants in April 1972. The order re-

strained Boise from employing a whole catalogue of sales techniques, not only at the four subdivisions named in the suit but in all 18 of its California projects and Incline Village on Lake Tahoe, just across the state line in Nevada. The sales techniques specified in the injunction included many of the tried-and-true subdivision hustles that Boise had been teaching its trainees as indispensible to selling lots.

The Superior Court's decision was publicly discounted by Boise, which claimed that the sales techniques specifically enjoined were already contrary to company policy. Boise president R. V. Hansberger wrote at length to the stockholders to reassure them about the newspaper reports of Boise's legal difficulties in Contra Costa County and elsewhere. "The claims against the company are substantial," he admitted. "But we have quality products and we are selling them honestly. . . . We are fighting these suits vigorously. We are determined to continue that fight." Hansberger claimed that the charges of misleading tactics in the Contra Costa action were unwarranted because the supporting evidence dated from 1967-68, Boise's first years in the subdivision business. Hansberger neglected to mention that such tactics were still being taught to Boise salesmen at least through the end of 1970. Referring to the preliminary injunction, Hansberger asserted that "since our policies clearly prohibit unlawful and improper practices . . . we have not opposed such a restraint," despite the fact that Boise had vigorously, albeit vainly, defended the suit with many letters to the court and a 12-page document of rebuttal filed as recently as a month before.

Only a week after the date of the preliminary injunction, Boise received another legal blow, this time from a jury in Oakland. The suit was brought by two would-be investors who had purchased a total of 460 acres at Klamath River Ranchos, a Boise development in Siskiyou County, in 1968 and 1969. According to one of the plaintiffs, when he arrived at Klamath River Ranchos after a free breakfast and plane trip, "Boise provided folk-lore, hamburgers, a fishing pole, and a jeep ride to inspect the property. The jeep was equipped with a two-way radio which created an 'auction-like atmosphere' for the sale of this land." The salesman allegedly promised that Boise would provide paved roads, electricity, and plentiful water; that fishing rights and access were included; that the land could be subdivided; and that Boise would handle resales. On the basis of these representations, the plaintiff allegedly was so impressed that he bought not only the original 20-acre parcel, but also an adjoining 120 acres that, unknown to the plaintiff, was in fact owned by the salesman in his wife's name; and still another 320 acres. The plaintiff's allegations of misleading sales claims were supported by other lot purchasers, and they produced a land appraiser who testified that the land they had bought was "junk" worth $30 to $40 an acre.

Boise claimed in defense that the land was actually worth more than the $175 to $875 an acre the plaintiff had paid; that Boise did not know of its salesman's ownership of the land; that the salesman was not authorized to make the promises he did. Finally Boise claimed, in effect, that the plaintiffs were well-educated people and should have known better. The jury ordered Boise to refund the more than $43,000 it had collected from the plaintiffs, and assessed Boise the sum of $500,000 in punitive damages.

The half-million-dollar damage award was later set aside as excessive, but it was not simply the amount that hurt Boise. The precedents set by the lawsuits, and the limitations put on sales practices, made it increasingly difficult and risky for Boise to do business. Resistance by some alert local authorities made new subdivisions tortuous and more expensive to undertake, and unfavorable publicity and full-disclosure requirements made them harder to market. And the more Boise tried to go legit, to provide more and more valuable amenities to encourage sales to people who would build and move in, the worse the situation became: front-end costs mounted high—as at Lake Wildwood—while fewer and fewer of the middle-income customers that the subdivisions might attract could afford to swallow the expensive bait.

The result was a complete turnaround in Boise's corporate fortunes. From a net income of $84 million in 1969, Boise fell to a net loss of $85 million in 1971. A 1969 net income per share of $2.85 turned into a per-share loss of $2.74 in 1971. The price of Boise Cascade stock fell from a 1969 high of $80 all the way to a low of $9 in early 1973—a paper loss exceeding $2 billion on more than 30 million shares. Among the shareholders least pleased by the debacle were some who had received their Boise stock in a 1969 merger. By June 1972, the Boise stock they had accepted in exchange for their shares in the acquired company had cooled from $74.50 to $13. They brought suit against Boise and its accountant for a whole list of improper activities, charging that phony accounting practices had been used, the truth suppressed, and investments made in an improper manner. Moreover, the suit alleged, "The practices and business methods followed by Boise in the development and marketing of its recreational properties were improper, fraudulent, and false, as a consequence of which Boise was, at the time of the merger, and remains, exposed to substantial civil liability with the possibility of recision of land sales," all of which "would materially impair Boise's business and its ability to market its recreational properties to the public."

For the stockholders, however, the worst was yet to come. After two years of increasing losses from its subdivision operations, Boise in July 1972 announced that it was pulling out of the business completely. To finance its extrication, Boise was putting up a special charge of $200 million against income. At the end of the year, Boise settled six of the lawsuits against it for $58.5 million. Of this sum, $24 million was to be returned to dissatisfied lot owners, $21 million was to be spent on administration and maintenance of its orphaned subdivisions, and the remaining $13 million was to be spent to complete facilities at some projects. The decision was announced by Boise jointly with California attorney general Evelle Younger, Contra Costa County D.A. William O'Malley, and the district attorney of Nevada County, Harold Berliner. The three had finally succeeded in bringing to a close Boise's five-year fling in the land-subdivision business. In that time, Boise Cascade had sold $360 million worth of lots in 19 California subdivisions to 40,000 buyers.

Busily selling off $100 million of its healthier assets to pay its debts, Boise could only claim that its problems were not of its own making. Robert Hansberger's last message to the stockholders blamed subdivision losses on "additional ecological safeguards" added to projects "in response to the upsurge in environmental concern," and other expensive goodwill offerings. For his part, Nevada County D.A. Harold Berliner took some personal satisfaction in Boise's defeat, a landmark in his long fight against subdividers in his county, and he had a simpler, not completely uncharitable explanation for Boise's debacle: "They thought they could take a pirates' business and make it legitimate. They had two choices— act like pirates or get out. For a while they acted like pirates, then they got out."

11.
ITT's
Florida Follies

While the pioneering subdividers in the West are staking out the last frontier, ITT Community Development Corporation is carving up a big piece of the remaining natural landscape in Florida, the 20th-century promoters' first resort. In rural Flagler County—487 square miles in northeastern Florida with a population of 4,454—ITT's Palm Coast operation is selling space for 750,000 people on 156 square miles, equal to almost a third of the county's area.

Palm Coast clearly looms large in Flagler County, but it is not immediately obvious how Flagler County can count for much in the conglomerate universe of ITT. With annual worldwide sales of $8.5 billion and installations in 70 countries employing 400,000 workers, ITT is the ninth largest industrial corporation in the United States. It sells everything from

sophisticated electronic communications equipment
to a dietary disaster called Hostess Twinkies, from
telephones to hotel rooms, books, truck and car
rentals, houses, telegrams, paper products—as well
as house lots in the Florida boondocks. ITT's multi-
national business activities involve huge investments
in foreign economies, and ambitions to participate
with the U.S. government in making policy toward
such countries as Chile and Ecuador. At home, ITT
can afford to underwrite a good part of the cost of a
national political convention, while settling its anti-
trust problems to its apparent satisfaction through
friendly negotiations with top government officials.

With infinitely greater resources than Boise Cascade, ITT anticipates the same benefits from Palm
Coast that Boise hoped to reap from its operations in
California. Like Boise, ITT has a housing subsidiary,
the original Levitt & Sons, that could participate
profitably in any development at Palm Coast. (Levitt
is fated to be divested by ITT as part of its anti-trust
settlement with the government.) Better still, much
of the land was owned by ITT's paper-making subsidiary, ITT Rayonier; though ITT prefers to advertise that "we first had to choose the ideal location and
area. . . . Obviously, that choice depended on many
factors: climate, access . . . dynamic growth . . . great
natural beauty. . . . It is no accident that Palm Coast
is where it is." And best of all, ITT could have its
land and sell it too: Rayonier keeps the right to strip
the pulpwood from a customer's lot while he is paying for it. A CBS-TV report on Palm Coast estimated
ITT's potential total cash flow to be in excess of
$200,000 from a single acre it bought originally for

less than $500. "We can get a 20 to 30 percent profit margin in land development," enthused ITT Community Development's president Norman Young in 1970.

Guests at ITT's land-sales dinners have been treated to the same high-pressure tactics and misleading information—and mediocre food—that are standard at similar affairs run by less imposing entrepreneurs. More recently, there is evidence to suggest that ITT is making an effort to curb its sales people's more flamboyant tendencies in pushing Palm Coast. ITT seems willing to rely on its corporate image to reassure prospective buyers of its integrity as a subdivider, despite the Dita Beard affair and other smirches on ITT's escutcheon. "When was the last time a large corporation invited you to dinner?" begins the invitation to a Palm Coast sales party. In closing, ITT urges its prospect "to accept this special invitation, because at the very least you can say to your friends—'Guess who invited us to dinner last week.'"

> While flattering itself, ITT blandishes its guests:
> We are inviting you because we want your opinion of an important project we are undertaking in Florida. . . . We have asked a select group of successful people, like yourself, to have dinner with us. . . . We'd like your reaction to our plans . . . we'd like you to tell us what you think about our newest venture. . . .

Presumably, those who accept the invitation expect to break bread with ITT's president Harold Geneen or one of his high deputies, and discuss arcane matters of business and finance. The invitation makes only a veiled reference to a "land sales presentation."

ITT also measures its project against its Florida competitors' and finds theirs lacking. "HOW TO BUY LAND IN FLORIDA WITHOUT MAKING THESE 7 'I COULD KICK MYSELF' MISTAKES," offers ITT's January 1973 full-page *New York Times* ad, which goes on to imply that all the other Florida subdividers are offering the wrong location, the wrong climate, or the wrong something. "Only the immense resources of a giant organization like ours could plan and build a community of this scope. . . . We're projecting an investment of $750 million to make Palm Coast a living example for the rest of America."

ITT's posture of being above the subdivision battles that engage lesser land promoters is carried through in all its advertising and promotional materials. The *pièce de résistance* is an article titled "An Approach to a New City: Palm Coast," purportedly written by ITT Community Development Corp. president Norman Young and Stanley Dea, who is both director of environmental engineering at Levitt & Sons and ITT staff consultant for ecology. The article was published in the Spring 1972 issue of *Environmental Affairs,* a quarterly sponsored by the Environmental Law Center of the Boston College Law School. "This article so effectively presents the philosophy behind Palm Coast that we offer reprints," advertises ITT. Neither the advertisement nor the reprint, claiming the academic imprimatur of this "respected journal," mentions that ITT's article was labeled by the journal's editors "Palm

Coast: Pro" and was followed by another article, "Palm Coast: Con" by Helen Privett Bird, environmental consultant to Southeastern Environmental Services of Jacksonville, Florida.

In a travesty of academic writing that would be witty if it were intentional, the ITT article is footnoted with eclectic citations: Aldo Leopold's *A Sand County Almanac;* Calvin's 16th-century *Institutes of the Christian Religion;* and the *Journal of the Statistical Society of London,* Vol. 2 (1839). There are also casual references, by way of name-dropping, to such celebrated modern observers of the human condition as urbanologist Jane Jacobs and pop ethologist Robert Ardrey.

In his introduction, president Young (always refered to as "Dr. Norman Young" to clothe him in sheepskin) pledges allegiance to "ecosystem continuity" and "maintenance of all parameters of life cycles" and "a city more satisfactory in the ecological sense than ever before anywhere." He promises "only the best that our talents, time, energies and resources can produce. At Palm Coast," he concludes, "given the fact of biological synergism, we do speak for plant life . . . and we do speak for animal life . . . but most of all, we speak for man."

The text refers to "scores of thousands of words appearing in our technical studies," which presumably guarantee the ecological sophistication of Palm Coast's plans. While offering "a few insights into our thinking, our philosophy, our science," Drs. Young and Dea warn the reader "to keep in mind the alternative to what we are doing with our land.

If, as is certain with land ownership, our

land had been sold to independent subdividers, each of whom built a 50-unit subdivision . . . there would arise at the very
least 5,000 different subdivisions—unplanned, unintegrated, uncoordinated, and
without all our controls. Such an eventu-
ality would clearly be unacceptable . . .
typical of the American tragic city-building
past. There is another alternative, to be
sure. Do not build at all; but then how
would the necessity of shelter be provided
for the expanding population? . . . One
might as well prepare a dirge for America's
funeral.

These imagined alternatives to Palm Coast are as
specious as they are self-serving. ITT's Rayonier
owned the land before Palm Coast was conceived;
thus, it is in no sense "certain" that the land would
have been sold to independent subdividers. Nor is
it likely that "at least 5,000" other operators would
have found Flagler County irresistible, in view of the
fact that in the four and a half centuries since Florida's discovery in 1513, Flagler County has yet to
accumulate a total population of 5,000 people.

Oblivious to such considerations, ITT's mock-
scholarly article forges ahead to dispose handily of
such subjects as "Bio-physical Environment and Pollution Control," "Wastewater Treatment," "Canal
Design," "Tree Preservation," "Psychosocial Pollution," and "Modility of Community Growth." Some
examples:

Tree Preservation

Studies: Vegetation on the site was mapped

and categorized into nine ecological plant zones: marsh edge, beach scrub, beach hardwood, upland depressions, bottomland hardwood, cypress, upland hardwood, and pinelands. . . .

Solution: Palm Coast has been planned to save as much of the existing wooded area as possible. . . . Roads are staked out and specimen trees are tagged for saving before any clearing work begins. Commitment has been made to save a minimum of 50 trees per acre. Where trees must be removed, or where they unavoidably die in place, replanting will begin as soon as possible. . . .

Species Preservation

Studies: Plans are underway to conduct a detailed study of the nature and number of existing flora and fauna species in Palm Coast. The study will investigate such ecological parameters as ecological succession, diversity index, limiting growth factors, patterns of movement, etc. Of importance also will be the evaluation of methods and techniques to enhance natural properties of the land. . . .

In her accompanying response to the article by Drs. Young and Dea, based on visits to Palm Coast late in 1971, Helen Privett Bird reports that around ". . . the area of present development . . . the great preponderance of underbrush and small trees, including entire forests of oak and palm, have been bulldozed." As for Palm Coast's promise to replace any trees it destroys, Ms. Bird comments, "Of course, that would be impossible. I would surmise that less than one percent of the trees have been saved. Not long ago, the area was a forest so dense that one could not see farther than a few feet into it. It was breathtakingly beautiful."

ITT's professed tenderness toward Palm Coast's green, growing things is also belied by the notice in the forbidding text of the government-required offering statement, under "Encumbrances," that ITT Rayonier retains the right to harvest all the timber from any lot until the day all installments are paid and the deed is delivered—as long as 10 years from the signing of the contract. Not only does ITT fail to mention anything about replanting; it plans on leaving the stumps to be removed by the lot owner "at a cost currently estimated at $200."

The question of sewage disposal is also covered in the ITT article.

Wastewater Treatment and Disposal Study: A thorough analysis was made of Florida regulations and policies concerning wastewater treatment and discharge of treated effluent into surface water. . . .
Solution: Based upon these considerations, a tertiary quality central treatment plant has been designed and constructed. . . . A centralized sewer system is now being built to conduct wastes to the treatment plant.

In its offering statement, however, "the Company makes no representation as to the extension of the central sewer system to any other areas of Palm Coast [than those already served]." Moreover, if and when a central sewer system reaches his lot, the owner is required to pay a connection fee, currently estimated at $500, whether or not he has a house to connect. Some purchasers are required to pay an estimated $650 in monthly $11 installments before they even own their lots, in order to finance ITT's planned sewerage facilities. While awaiting central sewerage, "owners of homesites will be required to install their own septic tanks and related drain fields ... subject to the requirements of the ... State of Florida. ... The current cost of such installation is approximately $350." In small type at the end of an advertising brochure, ITT advises: "The Florida Division of Health requires a homesite to have either a septic tank or central sewerage. *At this time neither can be assured on all lots. ...*" (emphasis added) The offering statement advises:

> If central sewage [sic] is not available or if purchaser, after taking title, is prohibited from installing a septic tank on his property, the purchaser may, at his option, transfer to another available homesite of equivalent value, or be refunded his full purchase price.

By that time, ITT will have had the use of the lot owner's money for 10 years, interest free, while no mention is made of the "interest" the lot buyer has been paying all the while.

As for fresh-water supplies:

> Studies also showed that the Floridian Aquifer, which lies to the west of our property, would be adequate from a quantitative and qualitative standpoint to supply

the 50-60 million gallons a day needed to
meet the demands of our ultimate population. . . . Additional studies were also made
to determine if there would be any adverse
effect by [sic] canal construction on the
fresh water supply existing in the area. . . .
The construction of canals has not de-
graded any fresh water resources nor
should it result in salt water instrusion into
the potable water supply in the shallow
sands.

Helen Privett Bird reports testimony to the
contrary:

The District Forester, a man with many
years' experience, informed us that 'salt
water intrusion into most areas of the county has been the determining factor that
this county has not developed.' His information . . . is confirmed by the Bureau of
Water Resources of the Florida Department of Natural Resources. In a January
1972 issue of *Florida Conservation News,*
it is stated that both salt water encroach-
ment and salt water intrusion are problems
already and that development is a possible
problem in the area.

Hydrologist G. W. Leve, of the U.S. Department of the Interior Geological Survey,
stated, 'There is great difficulty in obtain-
ing fresh water from the Floridian aquifer
in this area because of salt-water contami-
nation. . . .' During visits to both of the
visitor information centers and to the engi-

neering offices, I noticed that all used old-
fashioned water coolers with a five-gallon
jug . . . instead of the more common circu-
lating fountains. My associate, Mr. Wallis,
tasted water from the spigot in the restroom
and found it to be salty . . . and sulfury.

The federal government's hydrologist also told Ms.
Bird that "if the canals are allowed to transmit salt
water, they could produce additional salt water intrusion in the shallow aquifer." In correspondence
with Palm Coast, the Florida Department of Pollution Control reminded the developer that it had cer-
tification only for three "entranceway canals" into
the Intracoastal Waterway, which is all the "coast"
available to lot buyers at Palm Coast. No permit had
been issued for the connection of ITT's proposed
40-mile canal network to the waterway, despite the
fact that access by boat is one of the main selling
points for Palm Coast's artificial "waterfront" lots.
"The effects of these extended bodies of water upon
water quality," wrote the Department of Pollution
Control to Palm Coast, "are subtle and extremely
difficult to detect in the early degradative stages."

Barry Lessinger, an attorney who specializes in
Palm Coast for the Florida Department of Pollution
Control, claims: "They purport to be selling property
in a community they have fully planned and designed and which is going to be an environmental
masterpiece, when the contrary is true. The planning has been poor, they haven't followed normal
operating procedures, and the property they are
presently selling, especially in the canal areas, is or
is going to be an ecological disaster.

"ITT has built some drainage canals in there in which water quality will never be maintained," Lessinger believes, and he, too, is concerned about "just how much that canal dredging and their drainage system have interfered with the fresh water supply in terms of increasing salt water intrusion." Says Lessinger, "We have studies that indicate that the adequate fresh water supply in Flagler County may not be sufficient for more than 100,000 people. ITT's hydrologist has admitted to me that the only way they can supply fresh water to the whole community is with a desalinization plant."

ITT's autocratic water operations in Flagler County are carried out by the Atlantis Development Corporation, a wholly owned subsidiary of ITT Community Development. Atlantis Development is chartered by Flagler County to manage its water, which, Barry Lessinger complains, "is the biggest ripoff of all. Under Chapter 298 of Florida law, a group of landowners was given authority to gather together to drain existing swamp and overflow lands. The requirements were that it was supposed to be a contiguous area; that they have a majority of the landowners or a majority of the property—that it was not a single owner; and that they comprise an entire drainage basin.

"Now, strangely enough," Lessinger charges, "ITT's Atlantis water management district exactly follows the contours of the ITT property, and gerrymanders out parcels that they don't own in the middle of the property." ITT's establishment of its very own do-it-yourself drainage district came after a stricter revision of Chapter 298 was already pre-filed in the 1972 Legislature. ITT quickly filed its application under the old law, Lessinger says, "and they got a circuit court judge in Flagler County"—where ITT reigns—"to approve it. It is being appealed."

So far, ITT has been able to protect its interest from challenges by citizens. "When the original lawsuit was filed by people who claimed to be affected by ITT's water-management district," Lessinger recalls, "the state moved to intervene, to file an *amicus curiae* brief. But that was denied by the court. When you move to file an *amicus curiae* brief, the general procedure is that the court will allow it if you can show an interest in any way, shape or form. Somehow, the court found that the state didn't have an interest." Curiously—or perhaps not—the court that found no state interest in such a basic water-management question sits in ITT's Flagler County fiefdom.

"At the present time," Lessinger says, "the state is just hanging in there, waiting to see what happens in the present lawsuit. The big key to this thing is this drainage district: if it stands up in a series of court suits, ITT will probably be able to proceed willy-nilly, any way they damn well please."

While court suits pend and canal-dredging operations are suspended, Palm Coast goes right on selling lots, invoking the ITT monogram to inspire public trust. Barry Lessinger comments: "Somebody from out of the state of Florida doesn't know anything about General Development or GAC or any of the others, and so they do a little bit more research. But the public looks at ITT, one of the biggest companies in the world, and says, 'They're right there in the public eye. How can they get into any difficulty?' "

PART THREE

Mortgaging the future

12.
The best
laid plans

ITT's Palm Coast is not the only installment lot-sale operation that pretends to be a planned community. There is hardly a hip promoter who does not claim that his inappropriate or premature subdivision is really the city of tomorrow, endowed by its creator with all the features beloved of urban planners. Thus, AMREP trumpets Rio Rancho Estates as "a scientifically master-planned community," while Palm Coast boasts "every inch of land use planned down to the smallest detail before a shovel ever touched the ground." GAC's billboards proclaim the "new town" of Rio Rico in Arizona, and "the planned 'now town' of Poinciana" in Florida.

In appropriating such fashionable phrases as "new town" and "planned development" for their land promotions, the retail land salesmen assume a mantle of professional legitimacy and virtue. They proclaim themselves to be in the front rank of those seeking solutions to the "urban crisis," to be on the new frontier, the cutting edge of the newest social technology in town. To justify its "truly new city" in Florida's rural outback, ITT Community Development's president refers to "estimates that in a 10-year period in the United States, in order to replace inadequate housing and build the new housing required by our expanding population, some 31 million new units are required." ITT's academic essay pontificates that "planning is a pragmatic combination of researches ... Planning is reacting with intelligence to consumer demand typologies ... Add to this the assistance of those steeped in planning experience ... people who have learned in the pressure cooker of practical problems."

Likewise, AMREP's vice president and general counsel, Solomon H. Friend, advised the federal Environmental Protection Agency that projects like Rio Rancho Estates "will significantly advance the Government's policy of dispersing people from congested population centers into new communities." And Preferred Equities Corporation, promoting the strategic virtues of its "master-planned" Calvada Valley subdivision, as convenient to Death Valley as to Las Vegas, mentions that:

> The President of the United States, in a recent report to Congress, said, 'Only a system of satellite cities, or completely new towns, can supply the living space needed in the United States. To accommodate everyone we will have to build a new city

the size of Tulsa, Dayton or Jersey City
every 30 days for the next 30 years....'
Certainly there is room for some differences in the
definition of a planned community. The concept has
taken different concrete forms in a number of new
towns in Europe and England. In the United States,
the new-town idea has been in vogue among planners
and government agencies in recent years, without
attracting enough government cash or commitment
to become a major element in American urban
growth. Nevertheless, we are not without some experience with new towns. Even as long ago as 1733,
the city of Savannah, Georgia, was established by
James Oglethorpe in a carefully chosen location with
a plan for growth in modular units, generous open
spaces, adequate public and community facilities,
and local industry. Other colonial cities were endowed from the start with similar amenities, inspired
by European new-town theories and experiments
which Renaissance planners derived in turn from
ancient models. In our own time, such planned new
cities as Columbia, Maryland, and Reston, Virginia,
are generally recognized as promising attempts to
create humane, self-sufficient urban environments
from scratch.

Even without a precise formula, and with the assurance that different circumstances will require different solutions, certain general criteria for modern,
planned new communities have been established.
Professor Philip David, who teaches in the Department of Urban Studies and Planning at M.I.T. and
consults with governments and private industry on
new-town development, told a 1971 conference of

the American Institute of Architects that "the new community is differentiated from a large subdivision" by certain characteristics, among them:

- The plan will provide for diversified and balanced land uses for residential, communal and industrial purposes.
- The project will include extensive amenities and public facilities, including facilities for health, education, social services, recreation and transportation.
- It will provide the residents with a choice of owning or renting a wide mix of housing.
- It will provide for housing within the means of low and moderate income families, and produce a mixed racial population.
- The project will create the atmosphere of a town or city by means of land uses that are mixed in both scale and purpose, and by providing adequate services for a self-sufficient community.
- The new community will include innovative technology, such as advanced systems for internal transportation and utility delivery.
- It will usually employ cluster zoning to assure adequate and well-planned open space for the entire community. Such items as pedestrian and bicycle paths, and the separation of people from cars, are part of this open space planning.
- It will provide a generous amount of green space and open land as a result of cluster zoning.

The federal government's Housing and Urban Development Acts of 1968 and 1970, which promise support for truly innovative new-town efforts, require many of these commonly accepted characteristics: open space, industry, racial and economic mix.

Certainly in any recipe for a new-town project one essential ingredient is money, lots of it, in advance. The huge front-end investment is needed not simply to buy land, which is only a small part of the cost, but also to support meticulous planning studies and the expensive "infrastructure" of roads, utilities and services that are in place before the land is sold for home construction. Reston, Virginia, for instance, one of the first of the modern planned communities in the U.S., was begun in 1962 for completion 20 years later. It is planned for 80,000 residents in seven villages, each with its own community center, on a total area of 6,750 acres. Reston's 25,000 households are to be matched by 24,500 on-site jobs. Five years and $15 million after work began, however, Reston's original developer, Robert E. Simons, was out of money, and the project was taken over by his backer, the Gulf Oil Corporation. A total of $40 million was finally invested before Gulf-Reston began earning any of its front-end money back. By 1973, 10 years after its inception, the project was in the black.

The new town of Columbia, Maryland, which shares Reston's strategic proximity to Washington, D.C., also shares Reston's ambition to provide a complete, self-contained community. For a projected population of 110,000 on 15,000 acres by 1981, developer James W. Rouse raised $100 million in front money from a group of major financial institutions.

Despite their easy lip-service to the new-town concept, the promotional subdividers are clearly not in the same league as the developers of Columbia and Reston. For example, Rio Rancho Estates' almost 100,000 acres, if they are ever fully developed, will accommodate several hundred thousand people. Yet in its first 10 years of operation there, AMREP claims to have spent a total of less than $20 million on planning, engineering, roads, utilities, even a golf course; far less than Reston or Columbia had to spend on real planned communities for much smaller populations, on much smaller tracts of land, and with far higher environmental standards. The same comparison would apply to Horizon's claim of "over $30,000,000 ploughed into improvements" on its vast subdivisions totalling several hundred thousand acres in the Southwest. Thirty million dollars is a lot of money, but spread over that much desert it doesn't go very far.

For all their pious pretenses, the "planned communities" of the promotional subdivisions are neither planned, nor communities. They are lot-sale operations, pure and simple. Their "planners" never commit themselves to a completion date, because they cannot. The development of the vast outback behind the flashy facade of the core area awaits the individual decisions of thousands or tens of thousands of far-flung lot owners, almost all of whom bought on speculation. The insatiable demand for land, assured by the promoter, will be a long time coming. Meanwhile, without any commitment to install improvements in advance to stimulate the anticipated market, no community of any sort is likely to be born on the scale projected by the promoter. The settlers in the densely built-up centers of Cape Coral and Port Charlotte in Florida, or Rio Rancho Estates in New Mexico, or Lake of the Pines in California, may take full advantage of the facilities the promoters have provided for window dressing. But most of the subdivision will probably lie fallow forever.

While the lot-sellers represent themselves as community planners, the actual effect of their operations is often to preclude rational planning by existing communities in the area, making it difficult or impossible for them to decide their own futures. Former district attorney Harold Berliner describes the effect on local planning of unplanned, inappropriate subdivisions in Nevada County, California:

In 1964 the county decided to develop a general plan to help chart its development to 1990. After a great deal of effort and controversy, one was adopted in early 1967. . . . Just about all the lots authorized since the adoption of the plan have been placed in spots not contemplated by the plan for subdivision development. When public objection to this procedure started to grow strong, the supervisors simply modified the general plan to fit the needs of the promoters on their request. This had the interesting result of changing the general plan from one which would accommodate 12,500 people in eastern Nevada County by 1990, to one which would accommodate about 55,000 by 1970. No argument was made by anyone that the present population of 2,500 in that area was going to increase by anything but hopes and guesses.

Berliner's Nevada County includes part of the Lake Tahoe Basin, where pell-mell subdivision has compromised one of the most ambitious and sophisticated land-use plans ever attempted in the United States. The alpine basin has become the arena for a contest between those who favor the uninhibited exploitation of the area and those who would try to preserve the unique natural beauty that remains.

Sporadic unsuccessful attempts have been made to preserve the Tahoe basin ever since its recovery from rapacious timbering in the post-Civil War mining boom. In the absence of adequate protection for the pure lake on the California-Nevada border, development was accelerated by the introduction of legal gambling on the Nevada shore after World War II. South Lake Tahoe became a little Las Vegas: between 1958 and 1968, the city's gambling revenues increased fivefold from $14.4 million to $62.5 million. The basin's long, recuperative winter sleeps were ended forever when promoters attracted the 1960 Winter Olympic Games to nearby Squaw Valley, touching off a ski boom. Under growing pressure from recreational and residential development, assessed property values at the north end of Lake Tahoe rose from $20.8 million in 1960 to $119.8 million only 10 years later.

Under the aegis of permissive local regulations, Tahoe has become a subdividers' paradise. Huge new-style conglomerates, old-line companies and independent operators elbow each other around the pristine lake. The corporate landlords include Southern Pacific, Fiberboard, and Boise Cascade at the north end; and Gulf Oil, Dillingham and Redstone Mining at the south. Walls of condominium apartments and tall gambling hotels crowd the water's edge. Any chance that the basin might achieve National Park status has been forfeited forever, despite the persistent efforts of some residents and the unique splendor of the Tahoe landscape.

After years of local effort, however, a Tahoe Regional Planning Agency was formed in March 1970 by merging separate Nevada and California planning bodies. The bi-state compact, ratified by Congress, states that:

> The waters of Lake Tahoe and other resources of the Lake Tahoe region are threatened with deterioration or degeneration, which may endanger the natural beauty and economic productivity of the region ... the region is experiencing problems of resource use and deficiencies of environmental control ... there is a need to maintain an equilibrium between the region's natural endowment and its manmade environment, to preserve the scenic beauty and recreational opportunities of the region ... it is imperative that there be established an areawide planning agency with power to adopt and enforce a regional plan of resource conservation and orderly development, to exercise effective environmental controls.

Crippled by political bickering, the Tahoe Regional Planning Agency nevertheless managed to complete an extensive and extraordinary land capability study of the entire basin. The area was divided by a grid into 22,000 sections. Computers at Berkeley profiled each 10-acre section in terms of 59 variables of topography, climate, soils, vegetation and hydrology. From this data, the land-use capability of each section was rated on a scale of 1 to 7, from "conservation"—no development—to "urban services"—intensive development.

The resulting land-use plan allowed a maximum population for the basin of 134,000 people, less than its current population on a summer weekend. But under pressure from aroused development forces, the original work of the planning agency was supplanted by a more permissive plan allowing a maximum population of 280,000.

The opposition that forced the doubling of Tahoe's maximum population was only one of the frustrations that confronted the basin's planners. Far more crippling was the legal necessity to exempt all existing subdivisions from regulation by means of a "grandfather clause." No one even pretends to know precisely how many vacant lots have been grandfathered around Lake Tahoe, waiting like time bombs to be developed in the indefinite future without regard to any land-use policies. One county supervisor's sanguine estimate of 30,000 latent subdivision lots in El Dorado County alone—"enough lots to support roughly a population of 120,000 people"—illustrates the potential for the continued exploitation of the fragile Tahoe basin, and the futility of even the most enlightened and sophisticated planning in areas beset by inappropriate subdivisions.

In the rural counties favored by subdividers looking for cheap land, local planning boards are often overwhelmed by the promoters' grand promises, elaborate plans, and apparent expertise. In some cases, however, there is no planning capability of any kind to inconvenience the subdividers. When ITT Community Development proposed to subdivide one-third of Flagler County, Florida, for 750,000 people, "there was absolutely nothing" in the way of a local planning authority, recalls Pollution Control Department lawyer Barry Lessinger. The county commissioners replied to one request for information on local planning procedures with the admission that "Flagler County does not have an engineer and most of your questions should be directed to ITT-Palm Coast, as they are the only people having the answers to most of your questions at the present time." Lessinger adds, "There is now a county zoning and planning board, but it is chaired by an official of ITT Community Development."

Even if no appreciable amount of construction ever takes place, the mere presence of a large subdivision can monopolize the landscape for a long time, preempting any real development potential the area may have. As Robert H. Doyle, executive director of the East-Central Florida Regional Planning Council, told *Newsday* reporter Robert A. Caro in 1963, "A developer sells to thousands of different people. Then he gets out. Another developer might want to come in and drain the area and develop it, but it's almost impossible to assemble property in which the ownership has been divided . . . all over the country. So the land may never be developed."

Around the town of Deming in southwestern New Mexico, for instance, Great Western Lands has carved 112 noncontiguous parcels of land, totaling 54 square miles, into a wasteland subdivision called Deming Ranchettes. For 13 years, the sales campaign for the land has been carried on in newspapers, including *The New York Times,* and magazines such as *TV Guide,* promising that Deming's desert flats will soon be the scene of an urban concentration to challenge Las Cruces, 60 miles east on the Rio Grande. The developers, headed by former New Mexico State Representative Carter W. Kirk, assert that "experienced real estate men call Deming a 'coming Las Cruces'" and "they've already begun to refer to Las Cruces as a 'coming El Paso.'"

But so far there are no signs of rampant growth. Deming had 5,672 people in 1950, and 8,343 in 1970 —a gain of only 2,671 people in 20 years, an average of 133 per year. At this rate, it will take more than a thousand years for Deming Ranchettes alone to be fully populated. As of August 1971—more than 10 years after national sales of the lots began—only 142 "residences" had been established on the scattered subdivision, and to a journalist looking for them over the desolate, wind-scoured desert tracts, a large percentage appeared to be house trailers.

Yet if any substantial development were ever to descend on Deming, as the promoter promises, it would be frustrated by the many dormant subdivisions that besiege the town. Land acquisition and planning prerequisite to any extensive development, public or private, would have to contend with the distant owners of thousands of ranchette half-acres.

13.
After the
ball is over

If promotional subdivisions were the "new towns"
and "planned communities" they advertise themselves to be, they would be boons to the surrounding
counties, and to nearby municipalities that are
chronically overtaxed and underfinanced. As it is,
however, promotional subdivisions only intensify the
plight of local jurisdictions. Even an empty "paper"
subdivision preempts the capability of existing towns
or counties to plan their own future growth and al-
leviate their own problems. But with even a few lot
owners in residence, future planning problems are
compounded by demands for services right now.

However, by virtue of the very fact that they will
not be fully developed for many years, if ever, the
ill effects of a promotional subdivision may not be
obvious to local officials confronted with a plan for

a new project by an enthusiastic promoter. Instead, all they see is the opportunity to collect taxes indefinitely on overvalued lots, most of which will not be occupied by voters demanding services in return until the millenium or after.

Dazzled, they do not see, as the Northern Environmental Council in Duluth, Minnesota, pointed out in 1972, that "these mass . . . promotions suddenly create vast new urban communities without adequate local government or public services." After the lots are sold and the subdivider is long gone, "left behind is usually a weak landowners association and the same rural township government to deal with mounting demands imposed by . . . homeowners who expect road maintenance, sanitary waste disposal, fire and police protection, lake and (often) dam management, and miscellaneous public services including schools for those who become permanent residents."

In December 1970, the California Senate held hearings on legislation designed to help counties control "premature subdivisions." Among those testifying against the legislation were the expected representatives of the subdividers, the real-estate industry and the home builders. They were joined by John M. Caswell, speaking for the board of supervisors of El Dorado County, which includes a large segment of the Lake Tahoe basin. In explanation of his board's opposition to the legislation, Mr. Caswell said:

> . . . El Dorado County approves many residential subdivisions primarily on the basis of recreational, second home, and ultimate retirement use. El Dorado County does . . .

not desire residential subdivisions ... to be rapidly improved by development.... We recognize that rapid development would only result in many problems for local government at all levels.

Under questioning by the senators, Mr. Caswell elaborated on the attitude of his county toward promotional subdivisions:

... there would be no chance that even in five years they would be anywhere near built out. Most of these [lots] are bought on a very long-term basis with a thought to the future, and are mostly retirement people, who do not demand services of the police or welfare or hospitals.... We feel the fact that these are not built out ... we think that's good. We don't want them built out....

SENATOR CARPENTER: What is your population?

MR. CASWELL: Between 40,000 and 45,000 for the county....

CHAIRMAN WALSH: What would you say in acreage has been not developed, but subdivided ... in your area?

MR. CASWELL: ... The last I knew there were about 30,000 subdivided lots in El Dorado County....

SENATOR CARPENTER: Do you find that your tax base has been supplemented beneficially ... ?

MR. CASWELL: Yes, we feel counter to what other people have said here, that we have benefitted greatly, because as I say, these uninhabited lots do not create [a demand for services] and I'm speaking of just the county services and eliminating schools. . . .

SENATOR CARPENTER: The values go up and the taxes go up, but you don't have to provide the other services?

MR. CASWELL: No, we're not providing police service. These people that buy lots don't go onto welfare or get in jail . . . and then naturally the other one is schools. . . .

SENATOR CARPENTER: So, over a 15-year period, your history has been that they are not developing at any substantial rate?

MR. CASWELL: That's correct. . . .

SENATOR NEJEDLY: . . . You can tell your people in your county when those lots do develop, you are going to have some real problems. . . . Even when these properties are built on and the people then are permanent residents of the county, you don't anticipate any serious problems as far as the cost of government is concerned?

MR. CASWELL: . . . We now have enough lots to support roughly a population of 120,000 people plus our 40,000.

SENATOR NEJEDLY: When you get that 120,000, what do you anticipate in terms of tax rates and governmental expenses?

MR. CASWELL: Maybe we should be taking a longer view, but we feel that it will never catch up with. . . .

SENATOR NEJEDLY: But the tax advantages ... are short-term tax advantages?

MR. CASWELL: We don't know when these will build out.

SENATOR NEJEDLY: In the long run a residential property will not carry its load taxwise.

MR. CASWELL: That's a correct statement if they build out.

The future shock that awaits El Dorado and other carelessly subdivided counties was described by supervisor Jack W. Schmitz, Jr. of Madera County in testimony before the California legislature's Joint Subcommittee on Premature Subdivisions in January 1971:

In Madera County, between 1950 and 1970, there have been 21,048 lots subdivided and sold ... enough lots to provide living space for 73,668 people, which is 4½ times our present population. ...

Land values have soared, making the traditional farming and cattle enterprises not profitable. Low appraisals by the county assessor have not reflected the values paid by the lot buyers, causing a crisis in county government as we strive to provide county police, fire, sanitary and other services to the few people who have built homes in these subdivisions. At last count there were less than 100 homes built in these 21,048 lots. Most letters from the buyers of these lots received in the courthouse, and there are many of them, indicate that somehow

Madera County is to blame for any increase in taxes. . . .

We have a general plan and our county is completely zoned. We do have a comprehensive zoning ordinance correlated to the general plan. We do have a parcel map ordinance. We do have a fairly good subdivision ordinance. However, each of the aforementioned ordinances has an *escape clause*. If anyone is not happy with applying these regulations to their project, the Board of Supervisors may be—and usually is—petitioned to grant a *variance* from the regulations of the ordinance. The makeup of each board of supervisors dictates the effectiveness of the ordinance. Sewer and water systems, as well as roads, public utilities (power and lights) and other environmental improvements, are expensive, and my experience tells me there are but a few developers wealthy enough or willing enough to put their money on the line for a proper development.

From his long experience with subdivisions in Nevada County, not far from El Dorado, Harold Berliner anticipates the worst from the empty acres of a premature development. "Building a subdivision," he says, "is really the planning of a new city. . . . And the city's location was decided on by the developers for their own benefit. To imagine that the city won't need all the normal services is ridiculous. Although the building rate is pitifully slow, and the lots probably won't be fully occupied for many years, responsibility must be accepted for the fact that a city has been planned and may well come into being. In any event, it will not be 'cost free' to the county. It could become a real burden."

The prediction of ultimate costs versus revenues from a subdivision in any particular situation is an uncertain business at best, but there is evidence from counties and cities across the country to suggest that development is often more of a burden than a benefit.

Even a few pioneers on the endless acres of a subdivision can cause financial headaches. In Orange County, Florida, for instance, a study revealed that every 1,000 new residents include: 200 school children, 19 blind people, 67 old people, 11 juvenile delinquents, 16 alcoholics, and 30 mentally retarded children, all customers for costly city and county services. Such numbers moved the president of the Florida Senate to complain that the state's population growth "has strapped its treasury to the brink of fiscal chaos. State and local governments have literally depleted their fiscal resources trying to meet the needs of . . . new residents."

Similarly, the city of Denver found that each new resident was costing his fellow citizens $21,000 in capital improvements. A Stanford University economist's study of a proposed Westinghouse Corporation development near Half Moon Bay in California concluded that "by 1977 the development will require a yearly net subsidy of over $50,000 and by 1982 this yearly figure will rise to over $400,000. Palo Alto, California, after an analysis by the planning firm of Livingston & Blaney, learned that it would be cheaper for the taxpayers to buy 6,100 acres of foothills for $30 million and preserve them in open space than to zone them for development.

In 1972 city manager Herbert Smith released a study of the net cost to the city of Albuquerque of a new subdivision with full municipal services. For a hypothetical new 1,000-home project, the city found that its initial capital cost for services would be $455,287—52 percent of the total cost of the subdivision, and a loss to the city of $12,652 annually if supported by 4.5 percent, ten-year bonds. The city's budget, once the subdivision was in, would suffer a net annual deficit of $27,877 in operating expenses for water supply, sewers, garbage collection and other essential services.

The impact of unplanned subdivisions on Albuquerque is felt first by Irv Hensch, head of the city's Public Works Department, responsible for delivering services on an ever-expanding perimeter of development as subdivisions spread out around the central city. "Developing the perimeter," says Hensch, "means we have to reduce the level of services to existing areas to extend service to new areas. . . . The biggest problem is not only coming up with the capital to pay for these improvements, but the budget dollars. The tax base simply is not increasing as fast as the need." Looking at Albuquerque's 82 square miles of low-density development, Hensch agrees with acting manager Smith that "we should have more infill," as Hensch puts it, "some restraints on the sprawling effect."

In an effort to control subdivision sprawl, Hensch and acting director of city planning Vern Hagen proposed in 1972 a "Master Plan for Orderly Development." The basis of the plan was the designation of "development units" which would be "the smallest possible consistent with an efficient extension of the utility system." The plan envisioned the use of tax incentives to insure the orderly development of these units.

This official passion for orderly planning was opposed by the Albuquerque Home Builders Association, traditional ally of the subdividers. "Now is the time that all people engaged in the construction industry in Albuquerque should join together in this fight," warned association vice president Howard "Peg" Parsons, committing a $15,000 "research fund" to the fray. Nevertheless, the city of Albuquerque has been able to win a comprehensive planning grant from HUD to design a rational program for Albuquerque's future growth. The alternative to such a plan is clear enough from Irv Hensch's sensitive position at the Public Works Department. "There's such a thing as encirclement by improvement districts," he says, with an eye to Albuquerque's perimeter, where subdivisions are rapidly closing the noose.

Even if Albuquerque gets its comprehensive "Master Plan for Orderly Development," however, it will be compromised from the outset by the existing subdivisions, which already exert a disruptive influence on the city. These will persist in spite of any master plan, because they are already platted, and because for the most part they are outside the Albuquerque city limits. That even a peripheral subdivision can disrupt city planning is demonstrated by the recent experience of the Albuquerque school board. In

September 1972, Albuquerque voters approved a controversial $23.4 million bond issue for school construction. "It was hard to sell," reports William McMillan, who is in charge of new-school planning, because the issue included $5.5 million for an elementary school within Rio Rancho Estates and a new high school nearby. Although Rio Rancho is outside city limits—in an adjoining county, in fact—the subdivision was able to make good belatedly on its boast of on-site school facilities because it is included in the metropolitan-area Albuquerque school district. And "our job is to provide education for everyone in the district," insists Mr. McMillan, "no matter where they are."

The effect of only 1,100-odd households on Rio Rancho's 86,000 acres was to create a new center of demand for education. "There are about 400-plus elementary school kids out there now," reports McMillan. "There were only a handful a couple of years ago." Clearly, this new drain on limited capital siphons off resources that could otherwise be applied more efficiently, and perhaps more equitably, to improvement and expansion of the existing school system in Albuquerque proper. "If Paradise Hills and Rio Rancho weren't out there," McMillan admits, "we wouldn't be building those schools."

14.
Who pays
the piper?

While the city or county may find itself overtaxed to pay for public services in a nearly vacant subdivision, the individual lot owner will often be billed for costs that he might reasonably assume were included in the price of his land and his local taxes. Ingenious subdividers take advantage of an assortment of tax-like devices to make lot owners pay for at least part of the initial development, and for the future expansion and maintenance of facilities and services. In some cases, the customer is actually paying for the very improvements the subdivider promised as justification for the original price of the lot.

As in so many refinements of the subdivision hustle, Horizon Corporation was one of the innovators in this aspect of the business. Horizon's inventive device at its Rio Grande Communities south of Albuquerque is a fine-sounding but entirely self-serving institution called Horizon Communities Improvement Association, "a New Mexico non-profit corporation." The HCIA may be technically nonprofit, but it provides considerable aid and comfort to its inventor nonetheless.

What the HCIA does is collect dues: $10 annually from each lot owner. The annual charge is pegged to the Consumer Price Index, and constitutes a first lien on the property. Ten dollars a year probably doesn't seem like much to the individual lot owner; even the $370 over the term of the HCIA covenant may seem a slight addition to the cost of the lot. But on the receiving end, all those $10 checks every year add up. Horizon has 155,000 acres in its various Rio Grande subdivisions. Assuming that the entire acreage is sold in half-acre lots, the HCIA dues represent a potential annual income of $3,100,000, or almost $115 million over the 37-year duration of the covenant.

The disposition of this considerable income is at the all but uninhibited discretion of the HCIA, "which was organized by Horizon Corporation for the purpose of promoting and developing the common good and social welfare of the people of the community. . . ." The money can be spent for almost anything at all. The HCIA "is empowered to do any and all things and use its funds for any and all lawful things and acts that the corporation may, in its discretion, deem to be for the benefit of . . . the inhabitants thereof, or advisable, proper and convenient for the promotion of the interest of said inhabitants with regard to health, safety, education, culture, recreation, comfort and convenience of such community."

Under this broad charter, control of the funds is entrusted to a board of directors, which in turn elects the officers of the association. The election of the board of directors is seemingly democratic, with one vote to each lot owner. There is even a provision that Horizon's votes for the unsold lots it retains must total one vote less than the total of votes belonging to lot owners. As long as Horizon controls a significant fraction of the land, this one-vote margin of propriety simply means that if many lot owners out of tens of thousands abdicate their franchise, Horizon's bloc vote can outweigh even unanimous opposition from the rest of the electorate. Horizon need not worry overmuch about the possibility of a close call, however, even when most of the lots are sold. The lot owners are scattered all over the world, and election procedures are undefined. It is safe to assume that the HCIA will remain a compliant creature of the Horizon Corporation for a long, long time to come, at least until the HCIA self-destructs according to its charter on September 13, 2010.

In the meantime, the Horizon-controlled board of directors may use the money the association collects effortlessly, year after year, to subsidize any improvements to the subdivision Horizon thinks might attract customers, but which it does not feel moved to pay for itself out of venture capital or the proceeds from lot sales. Some of this investment might even be used to install the amenities implied in the original sales presentation: such things as roads, medical facilities, shopping, industrial development, utilities. Indeed, these are the very projects the association dues are earmarked for in the covenant.

In the process of making the lot owners ante up again and again for what they have already bought, the board of directors is empowered to accumulate funds from year to year; mortgage the community's public facilities; establish fees for the use of those facilities; foreclose on any lot owner for nonpayment of annual dues; and abdicate in favor of any successor it chooses or none at all. In short, operating through its puppet association, Horizon Corporation is free to collect and spend millions of dollars from its customers for Horizon's own purposes, without making any meaningful accounting.

Understandably, this device has been adopted and elaborated by other subdividers happy to make use of the extra cash flow while avoiding the discomfort of spending their own money for community facilities. Thus, by struggling through the lengthy small print in ITT's offering statement—but not from listening to the sales pitch at ITT's dinners—a New York City customer for a lot at Palm Coast learns that in addition to paying from $7,000 to $14,000 for a lot, he will be liable for:

• Taxes to ITT's Atlantis Water Management District "for drainage, canal maintenance, and for the preservation of water resources."

• A monthly fee of $10, subject to adjustment in relation to actual costs, "to assist in promoting the maintenance of the community and other purposes in accordance with the environmental and aesthetic principles of Palm Coast."

- A $60 water-connection fee, plus a $30 deposit for water and sewer service.
- $850 for "sewer facilities, treatment plants and central sewer lines and connections to buildings."
- "Membership costs and use fees" for the yacht club and marina, if he keeps a boat.
- "General and special assessments . . . for the purpose of maintaining and preserving the golf course and appurtenant facilities," whether he uses them or not. Fees for actually playing golf are extra.

AMREP, Horizon's neighbor near Albuquerque, has its own plan to pass the buck to the lot owners for supporting its "scientifically planned community" at Rio Rancho. While the original costs of building and maintaining such amenities and public facilities as the subdivision has to offer are being borne by AMREP, there is a limit to the subdivider's largesse indicated in the required offering statement filed in 1970 with HUD. "All common facilities are at present maintained by the company at its own cost and expense," the pertinent section begins reassuringly, "and the Company will continue to assume the costs of such maintenance until at least April 30, 1971." However, the statement hedges, "it is anticipated that an association will be organized by that time to which lot owners will belong, and to which they will pay dues sufficient to maintain such common facilities and pay for any other responsibilities assumed by such association."

But as of 1972, a year after AMREP confidently "anticipated" that an association would be in charge, there was still no provision for the lot owners to assume responsibility for the common facilities. There was a "homeowners' association," to be sure, but it lacked the participation of the vast majority of lot owners who were not homeowners at Rio Rancho and never will be; and it lacked the power or the inclination to exact dues. The head of the homeowners' association firmly promised that "we will not take over any facilities to take a few bucks off AMREP's expenses."

Other subdividers have worked variations on the same trick of shifting the cost of improvements and maintenance onto the lot purchasers. Among the most popular pass-the-buck devices beloved of the subdividers are "special assessment districts," "improvement districts," "utility districts" and the like. These are local jurisdictions legally chartered by states for the worthy purpose of giving unincorporated areas the same power to tax and incur debts enjoyed by municipalities, in order to insure them of revenue for the support of essential services. With his development legally constituted as a subservient special district, the subdivider can pass on a good many of his costs—including indirect sales costs—to his captive customers.

Ralph Nader's California study group reports on a subdivision whose developer promised that he would pay for "everything," only to leave his customers with an overwhelming burden of hidden costs. There was a $2,000 lien on each lot to pay off $4.5 million of special-assessment bonds; a liability for as much as 10 cents per $100 of assessed value to cover defaults on any lot in the subdivision; a levy to pay off a quarter of a million dollars worth of water and sewer bonds; a potentially unlimited tax to support $4 million in general-obligation bonds which could be issued without the lot owner's vote; and a final tax to support projects undertaken by the improvement district.

At California City, N. K. Mendelsohn used these devices in textbook fashion. According to the never-released 1969 report by the California attorney general's office: "The City and the district have incurred heavy debt to finance off-site improvements, and promotional and recreational facilities desired by the developer." Among these were a lake, golf course, tennis courts, and picnic grounds. "As of September 30, 1969," the report continued:

California City had a direct and overlapping debt of over $6,227,000, or a ratio to assessed valuation of 42.21 percent. These facilities were acquired by the Community Services District, which issued general obligation bonds and used much of the proceeds to reimburse the developer for his costs. The City has also accepted for maintenance 485 miles of either paved, graded or compacted roads that provide access to the subdivisions.... Most counties and cities would require that the developer assume a principal share.

The attorney general's report also profiled a classic case of this kind of deferred financing with the Estero Municipal Improvement District at Foster City:

Foster City is a 2,600 acre land reclamation and planned community development in San Mateo County. The district has issued and sold over $64 million in bonds to finance land reclamation, off-site improvements, a sanitation and drainage system, and various civic improvements. . . .

Residents of the area have been seriously disturbed by the voting procedure of the special district whereby the developer has been able to control the district and utilize it to obtain the funds he needs to effect the development of his land.

At present the outstanding debt is 258% of the county's assessed value. It appears that the market for Foster City bonds has been saturated and no funds are available to complete the reclamation and development project. As the tax burden shifts from the developer, who now pays 67% of the tax bill, to the homeowners, and as a higher proportion of the bond amortization occurs, as well as the inability of the district to sell more bonds to pay current interest, the district's taxes will become increasingly oppressive to the residents.

Foster City represents the type of tax trap that can occur in a metropolitan area when a developer is able to avoid the costs of development by translating the burden to the new residents, who must discharge the debt created by the developer's use of tax-exempt bond financing.

The attorney general's report concluded that ". . . it is clearly evident that a promotional district creates a disservice to its residents, to the community in which it is located, and saddles the area with obligations that cannot be alleviated even when the residents are able to seize control from the developer."

But there may be an even more insidious delayed effect of shifting development expenses onto the lot owners, especially when the majority of them are absentee investors. The likely scenario: as time passes, costs for improvements and maintenance rise. In subdivisions where the power of assessment is vested in a lot owners' association, resident owners control the vote at association meetings, and impose ever-increasing assessments to pay for improvements and services in which the absentee majority have no interest. If the subdivider still holds a substantial number of lots, he may support such assessments himself with a bloc vote. Where the power to assess is vested in a special district, similar charges may be levied to pay for expenses directly or through bonded indebtedness, again contrary to the interests of those holding lots for investment.

The investor group thus finds itself caught in a painful squeeze. Doubtless the value of the lots rises much less rapidly than the subdivider promised, if indeed there is any appreciation at all. More likely, there is no market at any price for resale. At the same time, annual assessments rise inexorably. At some point, the original lot owner or his heirs finds the endless and ever-increasing burden more than he can pay or justify. If he is still paying for his lot, he may decide to cash in his equity—only to find, of course, that he has no equity even after years of payments. His land simply reverts to the subdivider. Or, if the lot is paid for, he may find it attached for nonpayment of assessments that are a first lien on his property.

Either way, the process will tend to accelerate as fewer and fewer lot owners share ever-increasing assessments to pay for increasingly expensive improvements and more rapidly deteriorating facilities. At the same time, of course, county taxes are rising as well, adding to the burden. And assessments levied by a lot owners' association are borne in full by the taxpayer, since the Internal Revenue Service has ruled that such payments are not the same as local taxes, and thus are not deductible.

The potential for disaster is implied in the legally required property report filed by Sea Ranch, in Sonoma County, California, for all to consider before they buy. "THE SEA RANCH ASSOCIATION HAS THE RIGHT TO LEVY ASSESSMENTS AGAINST YOU FOR MAINTENANCE OF THE COMMON AREAS AND OTHER PURPOSES," the report states. "YOUR CONTROL OF OPERATIONS AND EXPENSES IS LIMITED TO YOUR RIGHT TO VOTE AT MEETINGS." Further on, in smaller print, the reports suggests some of the details: "According to the budget submitted by the developer, the monthly assessment for each unit is $15. *Expenses of operation are difficult to estimate initially and even if accurately estimated, tend to increase substantially with price increases and the increased age of the facilities.* . . . Any bonded debt or special district assessment approved after the . . . tax rate has been set could increase the future rate." As one indication of what lies in store, the report notes that "streets are private. The future care and maintenance will be the responsibility of the Association. . . ." (emphasis added)

Special assessments by owners' associations, special districts and other entities are not unknown outside the world of promotional subdivisions. They are an odious but necessary cost of living when equity demands that a public expense be borne by that segment of the population which benefits from it. But subdivision lot owners might reasonably anticipate that such a basic amenity as streets, for instance, will be paid for out of county revenues. Their own county taxes, after all, go for the upkeep of other people's roads. For the investor, who has bought property for profit only to find no market for his land and overwhelming annual assessments to boot, the prospect of eternal assessments for swimming pools, recreation centers and other facilities he does not use—on top of local taxes—may seem like paying for his own punishment.

15.
Conflicts
of interest

The promoter shopping for a subdivision site usually has a list of very definite specifications. To be attractive to the customer, the location should be arguably convenient to some existing epicenter of population growth: Miami, Tucson or Albuquerque, the San Francisco Bay area, the Boston-New York-Washington corridor. The land will also benefit from a reasonable proximity to some celebrated tourist attraction, either man-made, like Disney World or Las Vegas, or God-given like the seashore or the Grand Canyon. The subdivider can profitably capitalize on such public property as clean air, distant mountains, and other increasingly rare natural amenities. Even while endowed with some or all of these promotable virtues, the land should be remote enough from civilization, and sufficiently inappropriate for real development, to be cheap for the subdivider to buy up in vast quantities. By the same token, ideal subdivision land is often also ecologically fragile: deserts, swamps, mountain slopes, and other economically marginal landscapes.

For many of the same reasons that a tract of land appeals to a subdivider, however, it may also be a likely candidate for designation as a national or state park, recreation area or wilderness preserve. In such cases, there is a head-on conflict between the public interest in protection of the land, and the subdivider's urge to appropriate its special values for private profit. In some cases, the subdivider is able to thwart the public purpose entirely. For example, when the publisher of *Forbes* magazine bought the 168,000-acre Trinchera Ranch in the San Luis Valley of southern Colorado, reported *The Valley Courier*, it preempted efforts by the National Forest Service to acquire the land. "The hope of the residents of the county and the Valley had been that the Forest Service take over the land," the *Courier* reported.

In other cases, the presence of subdivisions has made public acquisition of land so expensive as to strain the government's commitment to preservation. Recently, the federal government and the state of Florida announced intentions to secure the Big Cypress Swamp north of the Everglades as a vital water recharge area for south Florida and Everglades National Park. According to a spokesman for U.S. Senator Lawton Childs of Florida, however, the existence of some 22,000 subdivision lots in the swamp inflated the acquisition price tag to $150 million, and almost sabotaged the project before it was fairly begun.

Sometimes a subdivider anticipates a public acquisition so closely as to suggest that his project's
sole purpose is to profit from the legal condemnation
of its lots at an inflated price. Such a threat preceded
the establishment of a national seashore at Georgia's
Cumberland Island, the largest in the chain known
for good reason as the Golden Isles.

The intent of Congress in 1972 was to add Cumberland to the growing list of Atlantic coast national
seashores—which already included Cape Cod, Cape
Hatteras in North Carolina, and Gateway at the
entrance to New York harbor—as recreation areas for
the public along the heavily developed Atlantic
coast. By that time the need for protection was clear
and critical. As early as 1954, the National Park
Service had surveyed the Atlantic and Gulf coastline—3,700 miles from Calais, Maine, to Brownsville,
Texas, the salt-water frontage of 18 states — and
established the rationale for federal action to save
what was left. Park Service director Conrad L.
Wirth's opening words in his report, *Our Vanishing
Shoreline,* set the tone:

> One of our greatest recreation resources—
> the seashore—is rapidly vanishing from
> public use. Nearly everyone seems to know
> this fact, but few do anything to halt the
> trend.

Of the 3,700 miles of general shoreline surveyed, only
6.5 percent, or 240 miles, was in federal or state
ownership for recreation uses in 1954. More than
half of this was concentrated in three areas—Cape
Hatteras National Seashore Recreation Area (the

first to be so designated), and Acadia and Everglades national parks at the northern and southern extremities of the seaboard. Neither national park contains much beach frontage suitable for seashore recreation. As for the rest:

> ... the findings show that almost every attractive seashore area from Maine to Mexico that is accessible by road has been developed, has been acquired for development purposes, or is being considered for its development possibilities.

The National Park Service recommended that at least 15 percent of the general shoreline be acquired for public use. There was, however, the report noted, need for prompt action: "Inaccessible beach sites, including offshore islands, are almost the only hope for preservation today. Even many of these are being purchased by real-estate interests for subdivision purposes."

Of the offshore islands the Park Service wanted to preserve for public use, Cumberland was number one on the list, "the best of its type."

> This sea island is thought to contain practically all the desirable features for public enjoyment. It is sufficiently large to maintain community conditions of its plant and animal life. Most of the beach is exceptionally attractive. It has fresh-water ponds. The dunes are splendid, and fairly well under control by vegetation. The ocean waters are warm with normally dramatic surf effect.
>   ... Fine live oaks, with rich fern growth

on trunks and limbs, and hung with Spanish moss, are abundant. Sea and shore birds abound; the island contains a good variety of animals. Fishing in the adjacent waters is excellent. With a climate similar to Florida but somewhat less extreme in summer, there are few places on the Atlantic coast where more days in the year favor being out of doors.

This and similar sea-islands along the coast played a thrilling role in the New World Adventure. . . . Archeological exploration may well uncover here facts of considerable historical meaning.

The possibilities of developing Cumberland Island for public recreation and cultural enjoyment are considered to be exceptional.

In 1972, almost two decades after the Park Service urged haste, and only after a five-year congressional battle led by Georgia Congressman William Stuckey, Cumberland Island was finally designated a National Seashore. The Department of the Interior was directed to negotiate with the island's landowners for 70 percent of Cumberland's 24,000 acres.

The main obstacle was one landowner who decided to go into the subdivision business. He was Robert Monks, a 39-year-old Maine millionaire who had recently lost a very expensive, self-financed primary campaign to wrest the Republican senatorial nomination away from Margaret Chase Smith. Before that, Monks had prospered in the coal and oil business, and he was one of the leading promoters of an abortive scheme to establish a super-tanker seaport on the treacherous, ecologically fragile Maine coast.

Perhaps feeling unrequited in Maine due to his political and business reverses, Monks took aim at the even more fragile but less well-defended coast of Cumberland Island. On 200 acres of the island, all of it within the designated national seashore boundaries, Monks established a subdivision and in November 1972 began offering half-acre tracts at prices ranging from $5,000 to $12,500. Aside from whatever moral hazard was involved in selling houselots on land already earmarked for government acquisition, Monks was also baiting a trap for both his customers and the Park Service.

Lot buyers may find out too late that according to the legislation creating the park, any structure erected after February 1, 1970, will eventually be taken over by the government, by condemnation if necessary. Undeveloped land might be condemned at a "fair market value" far below the artificially high price Monks is charging. Meanwhile, according to Georgia Governor Jimmy Carter, the lot buyer "would have to beat his way through remote woods" to his property, since the subdivision was offered "without roads, utility services or access to individual lots." The governor warned that "this land scheme will cause many Georgians to be misled and acquire lots that will be of little use to them."

Should the government be forced to buy up the hurriedly platted lots at the inflated subdivision prices, however, the price tag for the protection of Cumberland Island would soar. "I don't know what he can do about it," said one dealer in Monks's lots of the governor's attempt to forestall the subdivision scheme. "There is nothing we can legally do," a Park Service spokesman agreed sadly. "We're going to have to go to court to [condemn] it." Referring to the role of the subdivider in driving up prices, the Park Service official said, "We don't have the money now to buy up the remaining property we need. It's hard to imagine what it will cost two years from now." There was considerable speculation that Monks's purpose in subdividing his land was not to sell lots, in fact, but to establish a credible condemnation price for his other acreage as well as the paper subdivision in anticipation of the eventual government takeover. Governor Carter charged that Monks was involved in "an overt attempt to escalate the price of this land at taxpayers' expense. It is simply an effort to create artificially a development price on undeveloped land." And according to the National Park Service spokesman, "It happens in virtually every new national park area."

The federal government had already experienced this kind of spurious subdivision across the continent from Cumberland Island at Point Reyes National Seashore in northern California, near Bolinas. In 1959, when the Park Service first began eyeing Point Reyes as a possible national seashore, it estimated total costs for land acquisition, based on prevailing values, at a mere $7.5 million. Less than four years later, when President Kennedy signed Public Law 87-657 creating the seashore, the cost for land acquisition had nearly doubled to $14 million. By the end of 1970, however, the total expenditure for land at Point Reyes had risen to $57.5 million, more than

seven times the original estimate and four times the
expense allocated by Congress in 1962—and the
seashore is still not fully in public ownership.

Elsewhere in Marin County, in the same decade,
land values increased an average of 101 percent. The
assessed valuation in coastal school districts rose 217
percent. But the price of Point Reyes went up well
over 700 percent. The delay between the formal
establishment of the seashore by Congress and the
actual acquisition of the land cost the American taxpayers $30 million — not enough of an overrun
to make a difference in the Pentagon budget, but
more than enough to endanger political support for
such low-priority government concerns as parks and
seashores. The record confirms that the major factor
in the inordinate rise in land costs at Point Reyes was
speculative subdivision.

In August 1957, just two months after the Park
Service recommended public ownership of Point
Reyes as "one of the finest relatively undeveloped
natural areas on the Pacific Coast," 1,100 acres of the
area were sold for subdivision. As soon as the national
seashore proposal made its debut in Congress, the
new owners applied for county approval of subdivision plans that included a sandspit the government claimed was federal property and envisioned
as a major tourist attraction. In 1962, when the
53,000-acre park was approved, the government finally paid more than $1 million for the sandspit alone,
including back interest. In all, the subdividers were
paid $1.9 million for the unsold portion of their origi-
nal 1,100 acres.

The same subdividers in 1960 had acquired another 468 acres for development. With local sentiment running in favor of the park, the county would not provide a variance in road standards to permit access. The developers, allied with local ranchers anxious to get in on the profits, threatened instead to use an old ranch road that would have opened up thousands of acres of Point Reyes to subdivision. The only way the Park Service could see to keep the seashore from being sabotaged before it was even fully established was to do business with one amenable rancher whose property controlled the strategic right-of-way. His ranch had been assessed at $255,565 in 1962. A year later, the Park Service paid $850,000 for it, setting an inflated precedent for all subsequent land purchases at Point Reyes.

Others were not long in capitalizing on the opportunity. In 1965, a group of speculators incorporated as Land Investors Research, "to acquire for itself and its investor clients carefully selected land investment with high potentials for appreciation." The next year, Land Investors Research bought the Pierce Ranch—2,536 acres at the very tip of Point Reyes—for $1.7 million, with a down payment of $100,000. The following year, 1967, when the Marin County tax assessor determined the "full market value" of the property to be $1.2 million, the new owners appealed, claiming that it was worth only $800,000. Four years later, however, when the Park Service got around to offering $2 million for the land, the owners asked $7 million. Part of their justification for the increase in valuation—300 percent of their heavily leveraged investment, 6,000 percent of their down payment—was a consulting engineer's report that the ranch could be subdivided into 4,500 homesites. In one of its rulings on the Point Reyes imbroglio, the U.S. Court of Claims noted that "the Point Reyes project has, indeed, performed valuable service as an example of what to avoid. . . ."

Yet it seems that the Cumberland Island and Point Reyes experiences are destined to be repeated wherever the public purpose requires land acquisition and planning that conflict with the subdividers' single-minded interest in exploiting the land.

The battle is even now joined in the Adirondack Mountains of New York State. There, in an area of about six million acres—about the size of the entire state of Vermont—New York is attempting to establish a land-use plan that will protect the rural and wilderness values of the area for future generations. Indeed, a constitutional provision for Adirondack State Park specifies that the vast preserve "shall forever be kept as wild forest lands." With this mandate, the state began buying up land in the 1880's to protect it from the depredations of the timber industry. The area was officially designated as a park in 1892. By 1971, when the legislature finally created a special agency to devise a land-use scheme for the park, the state owned only about 40 percent of the land— some 2.27 million acres. The rest, about 3.5 million acres scattered throughout the designated park area, was still privately owned. The Adirondack Park Agency's planning was thus scheduled in two phases, one to cover the state-owned domain; the second, the private land.

Phase One of the plan was approved by Governor Nelson Rockefeller in July 1972. Its design for the management and recreational use of the park includes almost a million acres—45 percent of the publicly owned real estate—restricted to wilderness uses, with only limited access and development. Existing nonconforming structures are to be removed by the end of 1975. Motor vehicles are prohibited, except for essential official uses in the off-season. Seventy-five thousand more acres, unsuited for full wilderness status, are protected as "primitive," and 18,000 acres of watercourse are designated "canoe area." The largest area, 1,150,300 acres, is set aside as "wild forest," to be carefully developed with campsites, roads, boating facilities, and other recreational amenities.

The plan was drawn up by the seven-member Adirondack Park Agency in collaboration with the state Department of Environmental Conservation, which has jurisdiction over state-owned park land. The department's commissioner, Henry L. Diamond, is also a member of the Adirondack Park Agency. "We tried to strike a balance," he commented, "in keeping some of the land pure wilderness and protecting recreational opportunities." In endorsement of the result, Governor Rockefeller wrote to agency chairman Richard W. Lawrence that the plan would "allow full public enjoyment of our unique Adirondack lands while assuring strong protection for the fragile areas."

Unfortunately, however, both "full public enjoyment" and "strong protection," as well as a "balance" between wilderness and recreation, depend on planning for the private holdings scattered throughout the park, and on that matter there is far less harmony and singleness of purpose. The siren songs of recreational subdividers, promising a massive dose of economic adrenalin to the depressed area, have inspired visions of prosperity in local people. Even before the planning for the park was under way, such heady dreams forced a compromise in the powers granted to the Adirondack Park Agency itself. The legislature allowed communities within the park to preempt the agency's planning function by adopting their own zoning laws, whether or not those local laws conform to the agency's park standards.

By his own ready admission, one of those instrumental in getting this bit of home rule through the legislature was a former legislator named Hayward H. Plumadore, once known to TV wrestling fans as the Masked Marvel. Mr. Plumadore is also a partner in a group that sold an 18,500-acre tract near Tupper Lake, in a town called Altamont, which coincidentally has its own zoning code. The developer who paid Mr. Plumadore and his partners $1.5 million for the land is Louis Paparazzo, who planned to subdivide the tract into two- to five-acre parcels, call the place Ton-Da-Lay, and sell the lots for $2,000 an acre. Mr. Paparazzo hoped to have 22,000 second-home owners in Ton-Da-Lay. The population of nearby Tupper Lake, one of the larger villages in the park area, is less than 5,000.

Predictably, not a few local residents relished the prospect of being overwhelmed by the seasonal influx of part-time citizens. Local druggist and Chamber of Commerce president Paul Meader was sure that "Ton-Da-Lay is going to upgrade our our tax base. It will be good for our stores." Mr. Meader characterized those who opposed the subdivision as "super birdwatchers." With a worried reference to the power of the park agency, he insisted, "They have to let us make a living. We have to survive, and if they put a fence around us and say 'no development,' we're in trouble."

Others were less sanguine about Ton-Da-Lay. One Tupper Lake resident, Sierra Club member Bill Bentley, claimed that local boosters were so concerned with "just getting along that they haven't got time to think of the consequences" of a large recreational subdivision, with its impact on local environment and culture, and its need for tax-supported services offsetting its contributions to the local tax base.

Mr. Paparazzo's initial application to the Department of Environmental Conservation was limited to a water-supply system for the project's first thousand acres. A lawyer for several environmental groups opposing the development charged, however, that the limited water plan was "but the thin edge of the wedge" for a larger development scheme. "It is quite clear," attorney Robert J. Kafin wrote to Commissioner Henry Diamond, "that the applicant intends to use what may be the least objectionable aspect of his project to obtain approval of the whole project. There can be no doubt that if the waterworks are approved, the applicant will promptly construct them. Every successive application—for sewage, for solid waste disposal, for impoundments and stream diversion, for open-air burning, etc.—will be accompanied by a claim of hardship since the water-supply pipes will already be in the ground."

At a public hearing on the Paparazzo proposal, the developer maintained that his plan included safeguards for the environment in a "covenant" to be signed by each lot purchaser, promising that no more than 20 percent of each lot would be cleared for buildings, roads, or parking lots. Mr. Paparazzo also stated publicly that intensive development on the 18,500-acre tract would be confined to a 3,000-acre central area that would include resort facilities and an Adirondack museum that "will not be just old saws or pottery, but something more dramatic—photographs and film with audio on the lore of the area; something that will appeal to kids and parents." Overall, he said, only eight percent of the total land area would be developed.

At the hearing, under questioning by state Department of Environmental Conservation attorney Robert Harder, Mr. Paparazzo admitted that there was no guarantee that future development would not include areas he did not "now contemplate" subdividing. According to department officials, no complete plan for the development was ever presented for approval—only a "concept."

In August 1973, Henry Diamond, acting as commissioner of the environmental conservation department, refused to issue Ton-Da-Lay the required state permit for its proposed water-supply system. The project, he noted, proposed 300 homes per square mile, more than 20 times the density suggested by the park agency. Just two months later, developer Paparazzo went to court to challenge the right of the state to prohibit his subdivision. Earlier, Commissioner Diamond had noted that Ton-Da-Lay was the first and the largest subdivision scheme his department had encountered in the Adirondack preserve area, and it would be considered not only on its own merits, but as a precedent for other subdivisions waiting in the wings.

Commissioner Diamond's anticipation was far from theoretical; even as the case of Ton-Da-Lay was being considered, the next contestant in the New York subdivision sweepstakes was warming up to make its run for the money. The waiting hopeful was no neophyte in the subdivision business. It was the Horizon Corporation, the self-proclaimed "leading development company in the Southwest"; with vast holdings in Arizona, New Mexico and Texas; total assets of more than $221 million; and a net worth exceeding $77 million as of early 1973.

With a record of successful lot hustling in the Southwest, Horizon was prepared to move east into New York State, which Horizon's co-founder and president Sidney Nelson had left in 1959 to strike it rich in the desert. From the Northern Lumber Company, Horizon bought 24,345 acres in the Adirondack State Park near the town of Colton. Horizon paid $2.3 million for the tract—less than $100 an acre— in April 1971, with the idea of dividing it into 6,000 to 9,000 parcels of an acre and a half or two acres, to sell for about $5,000 each. Thus subdivided, the tract might gross Horizon as much as $45 million. Horizon proposed to invest in such saleable amenities as at least one 18-hole golf course, a ski run and ski center, a swimming pool, a motel, and a shopping center, some of which might also eventually prove independently profitable. Two wild waterways —

Deerskin Creek and Grass River—would be impounded to create three lakes.

Between Horizon and the realization of this ambitious scheme for development of the park land stood the state government, in the throes of concocting its plan for the park. As in the Ton-Da-Lay controversy, there was no shortage of local support for Horizon's ambitions. The town supervisor of Colton, Harold Buck, maintained, "We can't stand still, can't stagnate. The only kind of progress we can offer is something like Horizon." For Mr. Buck, Horizon's commitment to the area was guarantee enough of the result. "It will attract a good class of people," he said. "The riffraff couldn't afford it. It's not going to be cheap. Horizon paid much more than the going rate for the property. They must know they're going to get something out of it." Most of the objections to the project Mr. Buck dismissed as inspired by outsiders "like the smart university professors." Mr. Buck's attitude was echoed by some local business people who anticipated a pickup in trade when the development was in. "We've plenty of room up here," said Mrs. Gladys Coleman, a hardware dealer. "Let's share it." And like Mr. Buck, Mrs. Coleman attributed opposition to the fact that "outside instigators have upset local people. They're making a good living in the city themselves, but they don't want us to." According to Franklin P. Little, who publishes the area's only daily newspaper and four of its five weeklies, Horizon "would take over what is now wasteland, producing nothing, and make it into a multimillion-dollar source of new income, new business, new employment and new taxes for St. Lawrence County."

But according to Richard Grover, director of the St. Lawrence County Planning Board, "Over-all planning would be impossible with such a scar as the Horizon development on the environment." Grover charged that "they're trying to move in before we have a chance to draw up a master plan." Among his specific objections to Horizon's subdivision was its mountainous site, which he said would make roads impassable in winter snows and spring thaws. Replied publisher Little, "St. Lawrence County 'Planner' Richard W. Grover should be asked to resign or forced to resign, and the sooner the better. In the good old days, people like Grover were banished from their home states or countries and if they ever came back were arrested and put in a dungeon."

And in May 1972, *The New York Times,* which followed the growing controversy closely with thorough dispatches from David Bird, Myron A. Farber and others, took a position against the Horizon development in an editorial entitled "No Bargain":

> ... The threat to the local environment appalls many St. Lawrence County residents. ... But to others the project offers the shimmering hope of jobs and a flow of cash to a region that is none too flourishing.
>
> If this were the clear choice, it would be a hard one indeed, and one might well talk of trade-offs—a certain amount of environmental impoverishment for a certain degree of human prosperity. But there is absolutely nothing in the record of this type of land development that promises any such *quid pro quo* or, in fact, economic gain for

any but the corporation. The kind of developer typified by Horizon is not a builder of new towns or a planner of communities; it is a land subdivider, interested in the selling of lots, whether or not anyone ever builds on them.

... The few purchasers who do build, however, will properly demand the kind of road maintenance and other services that will cost public money and impinge on the environment beyond the original silting of streams, the cutting up of woods, and the damming of a scenic river to make artificial lakes.

The economic impact on the area would be far from favorable ... the aesthetic and ecological damage would be forbidding. Summer houses or ugly empty lots would replace woods that now shelter beaver, deer and grouse. A scenic river would forever lose its character. Open meadows would vanish along with their spring flowers.

While the *Times* was editorializing, Horizon president Sidney Nelson flew east from his seat of empire in Tucson to the aid of his newest outpost. "I'd be shocked if they didn't allow development in this tract," he stated. "It's ideal." Mr. Nelson attempted to mollify his critics by claiming that the area was not the most scenic in the park, and that it had been ravaged by over-logging in the past.

Mr. Nelson also made it clear that Horizon's debut in his native state of New York was a giant step both for his company and the industry. Horizon's Adiron-

dack project, he claimed, would be the largest subdivision of its kind in the state, and perhaps in the
whole Northeast, where opposition to land development was better armed than in the Southwestern
desert. "New York is a tough, sophisticated state," he
told the *Times'* David Bird. "That's why no major
developer is working here now." In the same interview, he also allowed a look beyond the immediate
Adirondack project into Horizon's ultimate day-
dream. "We would like very much to become the
premier developer in New York State," he admitted,
"and we hope this job will win us the approval that
will let us go on to other developments. It will give
us a good lead time on our competitors."

It may be too much to claim that the prospect of
the Horizon subdivision turned good men against the
public interest in search of private profit. But the
wealth and power of the Arizona corporation un-
doubtedly distorted the democratic process to some
degree in the economically strained Adirondack area.
Many local officials, responding to hometown pressure, opposed the park agency's draft of Phase Two,
which would limit development of the private lands
in the park. At one of a series of 15 public hearings,
a local legislator voiced a common complaint about
the influence of conservationists on the agency's
planning: "These groups—I will use the word 'do-
gooders' because we are in mixed company—do not
give a hoot whether or not the small man, the guy
who owns one or two lots in the Adirondacks and
who lives here year-round and has to eke out his
living by working day and sometimes night, lives or
dies or has his land and his savings slowly taken away

from him. And kid yourself not," he warned, "if this plan as presented is adopted, that's exactly what will happen."

When the private-lands portion of the plan was finally sent to Governor Rockefeller and the legislature on March 9, 1973, it became obvious that the stringent provisions for environmental protection had been significantly weakened. The park's maximum population had been raised from 1.2 million people in the draft version to about 2 million in the final plan, an increase of more than 65 percent. The current population of the park is about 125,000 year-round, and about 215,000 in the summer, so the plan provides for a ten- to fifteen-fold increase, which will doubtless be of aid and comfort to the high-density subdividers like Horizon. Indeed, by leaving plenty of room for growth while establishing an ultimate legal limit, the park agency has willy-nilly created just the kind of pressure-cooker climate the subdividers like best. "You'd better hurry," they can now tell potential customers with the support of the state's own plan, "because the land is running out."

PART FOUR

The rules
of
the game

16.
I'd rather do it myself

Premature and inappropriate subdivisions are so rampant across the country that it might seem the industry operates free of restraint or regulation. In fact, however, the subdividers can justly complain— or boast, when the occasion warrants—that they operate under the watchful eyes of their own industry, the guardians of Wall Street, and both state and federal agencies. That all these layers of regulation have availed little against flagrant abuses testifies to the determination and ingenuity of the subdividers. It also indicates the inadequacy of the regulatory response.

The industry's favorite regulation is, predictably, self-discipline. "Only spare us the burden of government regulation," the industry seems to promise against the evidence of history, "and we will police ourselves." A host of industry trade associations has been spawned to forestall any governmental response to public unrest. When the Western Developers Council was founded in 1970 to represent many of the big California subdividers, *The Wall Street Journal* reported that "one apparent—but unstated —purpose is to head off state legislation. . . ." By the end of 1971, an industry newsletter counted 10 regional and state land developers' associations, six of which had rushed into existence during the preceding year, when the subdividers were encountering their stiffest opposition to date.

The window dressing for such trade associations almost invariably includes a code of ethics, to reassure the public that the industry is keeping its own house in order. The Western Developers Council's code piously asserts that land "should not be disturbed without good cause and social need," and pledges its members "to help insure that the future needs of our Western society are met by improving our environment rather than destroying it, by endeavoring to meet those needs with the least possible impact upon that which nature has given us; and to help insure that the product of the industry is marketed fairly and honestly." Among the code's 20 specific articles, number 14 pledges members to "reject the policy of *caveat emptor* (let the buyer beware). Members shall make accurate and full disclosures of all pertinent facts and conditions in their advertisement, promotion and sale of land."

Similarly, the code of ethics of the American Land Development Association stipulates that:

1. Members shall make honesty and integrity

the standard in all their commerce with consumers, whether representations are oral or written. They pledge to avoid misleading property descriptions, concealment of pertinent information, and exaggerations in advertising. . . .

2.   Members shall make no false, misleading, or exaggerated claims with respect to the investment potential of the land.

Even if such pronouncements are intended to have more than public-relations value, however, the trade associations lack meaningful enforcement procedures or powers. While they effectively front for the entire industry, providing a facade of self-restraint and high moral tone, the associations have failed to attract even lip service from most subdividers, including many of the largest and most mischievous. The American Land Development Association, for instance, claims only 500 members, out of some 10,000 subdividers in the United States.

In asking to be excused from outside regulation, the subdividers often disarm their critics by crying *mea culpa* for past sins, protesting overwhelming repentance, and promising a future of contrite virtue. "In an age of consumerism, those things simply cannot be allowed to continue," insists Frank M. Steffins, the president of GAC Properties, disowning his company's long history of shady sales methods. "We don't feel that high pressure is necessary any longer," Steffins boasts. "We feel that the caliber of our product makes razzle-dazzle unnecessary."

Nevertheless, high pressure and razzle-dazzle have made GAC and its predecessor corporation,

Gulf American Corp., the largest lot sellers in the business. By 1967, the company was selling $114 million worth of lots a year, and coming up with an after-tax income of 20 percent of sales, or a whopping $22 million. GAC's domain includes half a million acres of Florida landscape, wet and dry, in six subdivisions; plus 55,000 desert acres in Arizona; plus 302,000 acres around the world.

Even in Florida, where the techniques of land salesmanship are as diverse and elaborate as the tropical flora, GAC holds the record for inventive lot hustling with unequalled success. "The fantastic Gulf American Corp., in its most fantastic operation so far," wrote John Hunter in *The New Republic* in 1967, "is selling thousands of acres of water to people who came down to Florida to buy dirt, and is doing so legally, open and aboveboard, at, so help me, $1,000 an acre. Which means these people ought to be awarded some kind of Nobel Prize for salesmanship." One Gulf American operation was described by a *Miami News* reporter as "selling faith—at $800 dollars an acre. . . . No roads. No schools. No drainage. No churches. No golf courses or country club. Just land."

Under the laissez-faire regulatory conditions of its early days, Gulf American was able to manipulate government agencies as easily as customers. Gulf American officials and friends, including the company's founder, Leonard Rosen, were appointed to four of the five seats on the Florida Interstate Land Sales Board in 1964 by Governor Haydon Burns, who later became a paid consultant to Gulf American. Such regulation became a euphemism for leaving the

fox in charge of the chicken coop. The Gulf
American-dominated board was able to quash dam-
aging staff reports on the company's activities. In
June 1967, *The Wall Street Journal* broke the story
anyway. The staff reports, said the *Journal,* "accuse
Florida's biggest land-development company of
grossly immoral and unethical sales activities. . . .
Specifically, the reports accuse the company, Gulf
American Corporation, of flagrant misrepresentation
in sales of land, of selling lots bearing specific numbers and then switching the lot numbers to other
land, and of concealing key information from the
regulatory agency."

If Gulf American was embarrassed by being exposed in public, the blush didn't show. Only the
pinch of outside regulation visibly affected the
company's behavior. Later in 1967, under a new governor, the Florida legislature replaced the Interstate
Land Sales Board with a larger, more independent
agency which promptly forced Gulf American to
plead guilty to five counts of deceptive sales practices. As a penalty, the new board fined Gulf American (a mere $5,000) and suspended its sales oper-
ations (for 30 days). In addition, the company had
to accept monitors from the board for several
months, and to refund some $2 million to dissatisfied
customers.

Although no Gulf American official went to jail for
even a day, the company began to suffer from regulation. The Land Sales Board stopped approving
Gulf American's new subdivision offerings, and voted
to renew its investigation. Although Gulf American
was able to get its guilty plea and the attendant pen-

alties quashed by a Florida court of appeals, grand juries in two Florida counties began to hear evidence against the company. Strong criticism of Gulf American continued to mount in the press. A *Miami Herald* editorial called the company "an embarrassment to the community and the state. . . ." Gulf American stockholders became uneasy as lot-sales income fell off sharply: from almost $150 million in 1966 to less than $100 million in 1968—a 33 percent drop in just two years. The $22 million after-tax profit of 1966 turned into the $1.6 million loss of 1968.

At this point, president Leonard Rosen and his brother-partner decided to exit gracefully. In just 12 years, they had realized a profit of more than $57 million on an original investment of only $125,000, which they had earned in a previous venture by selling sheep-wool fat as lanolin hair dressing. Gulf American's successor was GAC Corporation, a financial services outfit that was willing to trade $200 million in stock for its debut in the subdivision business as a full-blown giant.

GAC quickly drew fire from the California Real Estate Board for misrepresenting its properties and selling without a permit; from a group of customers in Arizona who claimed fraud in a $100 million class-action suit; from Hollywood, Florida, whose mayor accused GAC of using pressure tactics to get approval for a high-density subdivision; from Rhode Island, where the state forced a seven-week suspension in sales and refunds totaling $235,000.

By 1972, the Council of Better Business Bureaus, hardly an aggressive critic of American business tactics, found such a pattern of complaints against GAC in its local-branch files that it felt forced to act. According to the bureau's 15-page, August 1972 "confidential" report, GAC's operations have inspired "a consistent pattern of complaints based primarily on the company's or its predecessors' sales practices and its inability to fulfill the terms of its contracts." The report goes on to list 19 frequently cited "oral misrepresentations by salesmen" and "other objectional [sic] sales tactics" favored by GAC.

Small wonder, then, that GAC, like the rest of the promotional subdividers, would just as soon do without outside regulation, and professes a passion for self-discipline. In 1971, the company hired a new president and dismissed nine top executives. "It was just a difference in philosophies," said GAC's public-relations director. "The new president, Frank Steffins, wants total community development emphasized. In the past, the company emphasized unimproved land sales; Mr. Steffins wants to emphasize the development phase now." However, in the same breath the spokesman allowed that GAC would continue to sell lots at "cocktail parties" around the country— the sales technique that seems most calculated to encourage deceptive selling and misguided buying. "Yes, that will continue," the PR man insisted. "That's an accepted marketing technique used by every company." President Steffins himself told Morton C. Paulson of *The National Observer* that "the parties are becoming smaller, so we can give more information to people."

Another GAC spokesman, a vice president for public relations, was even more reassuring to Robert Cahn, environment editor of *The Christian Science*

Monitor, Pulitzer-Prize winner, and former member of the President's Council on Environmental Quality. In Cahn's *Monitor* series on retail land-sales problems, GAC claimed that its sales force "has been cut from 2,000 to approximately 550, sales sessions are being monitored by professional investigators, and services of salesmen who engage in misrepresentation have been terminated."

Despite GAC's protestations of reformed policies, however, there is evidence to suggest that the company's actual practices have not changed much. If they have, by the fall of 1972 the news had yet to penetrate the sales force for GAC's newest subdivision, the 47,000-acre Poinciana, planned for an ultimate population of 250,000 in central Florida. At a New York City sales session, there was the familiar old pitch for land to be bought, sight unseen, as a prudent investment. "Is Poinciana a smart long-term investment in your future?" asked a GAC visual aid. "You bet." The salesman, a veteran of Gulf American days, assured prospects that "land doubles in value every five years." A quarter-acre lot in the same area "went for $25 to $65 in 1965-66," he said, while "a one-acre lot sold for $27,500 to $41,250" five years later. Nevertheless, as GAC admits in a 1971 prospectus filed with the Securities and Exchange Commission, "there is no significant resale market...." Evidently, GAC's self-regulation does not extend to telling customers for its lots what it is required by law to tell customers for its debentures.

Even if GAC's new-found virtue does take root and hold sometime in the future, it will not help the tens and hundreds of thousands of people who succumbed to the old hustle and wish they hadn't. Of these, many are still in various stages of paying for their land, while others are already the sole owners of their half-acres. But still others have despaired along the way and simply forfeited their investments to GAC. In the first nine months of 1970, for instance, GAC customers abandoned lots with a total price tag of $63,303,000. The land reverted to GAC's inventory, and the installments already paid were retained by GAC. For all such victims, GAC's repentance, even if it proves to be sincere, comes too late.

One New York customer, hearing of GAC's widely publicized new sales policy, wrote directly to GAC president Frank Steffins in the hope of recouping seven years of installment payments. She told Mr. Steffins that she and her husband had been approached by a Gulf American salesman when they were new immigrants from Europe, unfamiliar with both the English language and American salesmanship. After a whirlwind airplane tour of Cape Coral and a dizzying sales talk, they bought two lots for "investment." She reported that some years later, when they tried to sell the lots through Florida brokers suggested by GAC, they discovered, as GAC knew all along, that "there is no significant resale market." Complaining that she had been misled, she asked for a refund. GAC's only response was to refer her once again to local brokers, who are swamped with listings for Florida swampland.

Another New York woman, an AMREP customer, did better by not trusting the company to do the right thing. Well into her sixties and dependent on Social Security, she had allowed herself to be sold a 10-year "investment" at Rio Rancho Estates. Her appeal to AMREP for restitution was accompanied by a petition for assistance to the New York secretary of state's office, where a sympathetic attorney leaned on AMREP in her behalf. After nine months of interviews with AMREP executives, correspondence, and even attendance at another Rio Rancho dinner at the company's insistence, the customer got back the more than $500 she had invested.

Such happy endings are rare, but exactly how rare is impossible to learn. The subdividers are extremely wary of publicizing their refund policies, evidently for fear of inviting an avalanche of applications. But attorney Barry Lessinger of the Florida Department of Pollution Control reports that ITT's Palm Coast has been making quiet refunds to persistent dissatisfied customers. Lessinger suspects that ITT's policy may be intended to forestall complaints to the state government, where the attorney general is empowered by Florida law to initiate a class action which could force ITT to refund all the money it has collected at Palm Coast.

The lesson is clear: the subdividers' seeming repentance for past sins does not extend to refunding the profits; nor is there any evidence to support their protestations that they can regulate themselves to eliminate shoddy practices in the future. The obvious question: if the industry cannot be trusted to behave itself, who should be its guardian?

17.
Fun
with numbers

One institution with enough influence to inhibit the excesses of the subdividers is the Wall Street community, on which the industry relies not only for the usual financial support, but also for credentials of corporate stature and integrity. But for too long the financial community, rather than use its influence to promote reform in the retail land sales industry, has preferred to bet on the subdividers. The presence of a vice-president of Chemical Bank on AMREP's board of directors, for example, is frequently mentioned by Rio Rancho sales people. Chemical also loaned AMREP $15 million. Other financial support for AMREP's land operations comes from General Electric, through its Credit Corporation, and the Ford Motor Credit Company. The heavyweight subdividers—AMREP, Horizon, GAC, General Development ("The Integrity Company")—flaunt their listings on the New York Stock Exchange, as though the Big Board were some kind of exclusive gentlemen's club.

Indeed, on Wall Street, where stocks are morally neutral pieces of paper, the promotional subdividers looked good in the go-go market of the 1960s. Buying raw acreage for a few hundred dollars or less an acre and selling it, still raw, for $10,000 and up looked like the next best thing to having a key to the mint. Prices of land-sales stock boomed, many of them to 30 times earnings. Clearly, anyone investing in a lot from AMREP or Horizon or any of the others would have done better to put his money in the company's stock instead.

There was, however, a bit of bookkeeping alchemy behind the land-sales companies' earnings, hidden in the technical language and small print of the footnotes to corporate annual reports. The accounting magic was so basic to the subdividers' apparent financial health that when it was belatedly and timidly questioned by the financial community, subdividers' stocks tumbled—some of them to five times earnings and below—even though reported earnings per share continued to rise. (There were other reasons for the drop in stock prices, but the financial press reported the bookkeeping dispute as a major cause.) AMREP's earnings went from $1.94 per share in 1971, for instance, to $2.35 in 1972, while 1972 stock prices fell from a year's high of $29 to $16 in September. General Development's per-share earnings rose 5 percent in 1971-72, while the stock dropped 50 percent in price. Horizon's stock, after reaching a 1972 high of

44¼ per share, fell to under 20 even before news of declining earnings dropped the price as low as 13— a price-earnings ratio of two.

The stock market's jitters were a reaction to the possibility of a change in the industry's chosen bookkeeping method, known as "accrual accounting." An obscure detail likely to be overlooked by lay investors, accrual accounting was the instrument the land giants used to goose the goose that laid the golden eggs. In broad terms, accrual accounting means simply that the subdivider can claim the full price of a lot as revenue in the year the lot is sold, even though only a small fraction of the total selling price is actually received during that year. In an extreme illustration, a $4,000 lot sold on December 29 with a down payment of $200, or 5 percent, will appear as $4,000 in receivable income for that year; though the $200 actually received does not even cover the original cost of the land plus commissions and other sales costs. Such counting of chickens before hatching ignores the eventual cost of obligated improvements, such as drainage and roads, which will entail heavy expenses for the developer in the future. At the same time, income taxes are conveniently deferred, to be paid only as the installment income is actually received.

The accrual method makes the company's stock look good by grossly overstating actual in-hand assets; but it also sows the seeds of a financial bust in the future. Costly improvements must be made, if ever, at a time when new sales are fewer and more expensive to make, and current income from ongoing contracts has already been counted in the year of the original sale. Also, although reserves are supposedly set aside from each year's revenue for anticipated contract cancellations, any unexpected washout on partially paid contracts will result in actual receipts far less than those already reported to the stockholders. Finally, by anticipating income ahead of receipts and leaving nothing to show for future years except more new sales, the accrual method obviously increases the pressure on the subdividers and their salesmen to hustle lots by any means.

Clearly, accrual bookkeeping also encourages subdividers to accept frivolous down payments, as low as five percent or less, while banks and other lending institutions commonly require as much as 50 percent down for mortgages on unimproved land. With a short-sighted focus on the customer's signature and down payment, subdividers also customarily forego elementary credit checks, preferring to sign up marginal prospects, report the total income from the sale, then sell the same land over again if the customer fails to fulfill his contract. With accrual accounting, the quantity of sales is literally all that counts; quality becomes an afterthought, as does the actual business of building livable communities.

The clear dangers of accrual reporting were not unnoticed by responsible members of the accounting profession. "Indifference replaced traditional insistence on proven credit-worthiness," wrote Dr. Itzhak Sharav, a certified public accountant, writer and teacher in the Spring 1973 issue of *Real Estate Review*. "The accounting for the sale, on the other hand, was characterized by 'speed and eagerness.'

It can easily be seen that with these accounting methods, continuous and ever-expanding sales become more important than the productive effort of land development. ... To a company hungry for reported earnings, the original sale is more rewarding than the subsequent long and tedious collection process. Since income resulted from the sale at the very beginning and since profits cannot be counted twice, the later receipt of cash does not add to the earnings picture. In fact, pedantic credit investigation to minimize future defaults by land purchasers may get in the way of improved income, because it will tend to prevent the conclusion of sales agreements with marginal purchasers. ...

Such responsible Wall Street institutions as the New York Stock Exchange and the Financial Analysts Federation, as well as the Securities and Exchange Commission in Washington, militated for a more accurate method of land-sales reporting called installment accounting, in which sales and profits are counted as the cash actually comes into the company's hands. In 1969, under pressure, the American Institute of Certified Public Accountants ordered its Accounting Principles Board to look into the question. The land-sales industry, naturally, was adamantly in favor of the status quo. As *Business Week* noted, "Few companies . . . could survive on a pure cash basis."

After three years of deliberation and wrangling, the Accounting Principles Board's committee issued a draft of revised accounting rules for the land-sales industry. Instead of the full turn away from accrual accounting hoped for by the subdividers' qualified critics, the committee recommended only a "moderate revision," a "limited" step toward reform, according to Dr. Sharav.

The draft proposal caused something of a furor in the financial community. Robert Metz, in *The New York Times*, quoted one anonymous CPA as saying, "In my judgment, the installment method of accounting is the best approach. In this approach, you record revenues as cash payments as they are received. This reflects most accurately, in my view, the economic realities of the business. The committee ducked this approach, and I think it did so because it would severely affect reported earnings for virtually every one of the land companies."

More specifically, Metz's source noted that "a number of companies in the business have learned over the past two years that it is not possible accurately to forecast cancellations. I am thinking of Boise Cascade, which wrote off over $50 million on its land investments, and GAC Corporation, which also had big writeoffs." In November 1972, Metz reported a letter from members of the prestigious firm of Coenen & Co. to SEC chairman William J. Casey, charging that the proposed new bookkeeping rules were an "arrogant financial accounting hoax."

There were also charges that Philip L. Defliese, the chairman of the Accounting Principles Board, "for almost three years has permitted the procrastination and compromise associated with the retail land sales draft while his firm's major land company client, the General Development Corporation, has been extremely active in opposing any semblance of meaningful land sales accounting reform." Defliese's firm, Lybrand, Ross Brothers and Montgomery, one of the "Big Eight" accounting firms, also handles the books of Horizon Corporation.

Mr. Defliese admitted to Metz that of the 18 members of the Accounting Principles Board, "six or seven" were from Big Eight firms that have land-company clients. On the committee that drafted the new accounting rules, four of the six members had such ties to the industry, representing Boise Cascade, Deltona and GAC, as well as Horizon and General Development. A fifth member was an officer of a firm with a land-sales subsidiary of its own. To guard against any possible suggestion of conflict of interest on his own part, however, Mr. Defliese announced that he would abstain from voting for the draft proposal unless a two-thirds majority of the Accounting Principles Board approved it.

The rule-making proceeded in what Metz described as "an atmosphere of considerable debate and even intrigue." The New York Stock Exchange, which had previously come out strongly for installment accounting, reversed itself in favor of the proposed modified accrual system, then settled for an in-between position of accrual accounting with some supplementary income reporting. For its part, the Securities and Exchange Commission seemed to remain firm. In a letter to the Accounting Principles Board, the SEC's chief accountant wrote, "In our view, the [accrual] method . . . does not reflect the business of the companies involved, is subject to a significant degree of manipulation . . . and will result in a set of financial statements that are difficult to justify within the framework of accounting theory. Most important, it appears that the accounting procedures set forth would be virtually impossible for the average informed investor to understand." In the end, however, the SEC too seemed to buckle, agreeing to accept the Accounting Principle Board's plan if it had the support of two-thirds of the board's members.

As expected, the APB voted 15-3 in January 1973 to adopt the modified accrual system drafted by its committee. In outline, the new rules mandate the use of the accrual system if the lots will be useable for residential or recreational use upon completion of the sales contract; if the company is capable of completing planned improvements and these are already under way; and if past experience indicates that 90 percent of the contracts in force six months after the sale is recorded will be paid in full. Sales cannot be counted as receipts until 10 percent of the price has been paid.

Even such easy-going restrictions will require more modest financial statements from most subdividers. Restatement of 1971 earnings, required under the new rules, has been estimated to require lopping as much as 20 percent or more off the earnings-per-share reported by many companies.

There is, however, at least one sweet solace in the new rules for subdividers who can no longer qualify for accrual accounting. In order to enable investors to compare the subdividers' performance in past years, the APB ordered the industry to re-report all previous years by the installment method. In effect, while making it somewhat more difficult to count chickens prematurely, the APB was inviting the subdividers to count them twice. Sales that have already been reported as receivables to inflate past earnings can now be reported again as income actually received on the installment basis. Considering the baroque intricacies of the new rules, an analyst for the Wall Street firm of Bache & Co. advised that "investors should stay away from these stocks for at least a year. It will take them that long to understand them."

Three years of doubt over whether the subdividers would be able to continue overstating their earnings had contributed to a marked drop in stockholder confidence. As the Accounting Principles Board was voting on its new rules, Robert Metz in the *Times* totaled up the decline in the paper value of seven leading promotional subdividers. The list included AMREP, Boise Cascade, Deltona, GAC, General Development, Horizon, and McCulloch. The total paper loss to the stockholders: $3.11 *billion*. Depending on the point of view, this was either a disastrous drop in value, or a more accurate reflection of the subdividers' true worth.

All the same, the subdividers had emerged from their trial-by-accountant in far better shape than many of their critics felt they deserved. "The accountants' committee," wrote the SEC's chief accountant, John C. Burton, "has struggled valiantly to try to develop appropriate accounting principles for this industry but in our judgment has not succeeded in doing so." A more succinct comment to the same effect came from Abraham J. Briloff, professor of accountancy at the City University of New York and the most persistent professional critic of the land-sales industry's accounting practices. As a dissenting member of the CPA's Committee on Land Development Companies, Briloff called the committee's purported reform "a fake."

18.
The law
of the land

If the industry will not regulate itself, and the financial institutions fail to curb its excesses, it seems reasonable to hope that the state and federal governments will protect the consumer from deceptive land sales and the land from inappropriate subdivision. For the consumer, legislation exists at both state and federal levels. Unfortunately, however, due to limitations in both the legislation and its enforcement, the consumer has been afforded little protection from any but the most blatant subdivision schemes. At the same time, the semblance of meaningful regulation has made the land-hustler's job easier by lulling the consumer into a false sense of security. As is often the case with other industries, inadequate regulation is embraced by the subdividers as their most credible defense against criticism.

Thus, there is hardly a lot salesman well educated in the tricks of his trade who does not point to the offering statements required by both the federal and many state governments and boast that they signify official endorsement of the subdivision. The claim may be made explicitly or by suggestion, despite the required disclaimer on the front page of the statement. In New York state, the disclaimer specifies that acceptance of the offering statement by the state "DOES NOT CONSTITUTE APPROVAL OF THE SALE... BY THE DEPARTMENT OF STATE OR ANY OFFICER THEREOF OR [INDICATE] THAT THE DEPARTMENT OF STATE HAS IN ANYWAY PASSED UPON THE MERITS OF THE OFFERING." Federal property reports carry a similar disclaimer: "This report is not a recommendation or endorsement. . . ."

Nevertheless, ITT's Palm Coast, for instance, reassures its prospects that "land developers in Florida are closely scrutinized by federal and state authorities." And the sales manager at a Rio Rancho Estates dinner in New York soothes:

Right now I would like to furnish you with a fact that I feel is extremely important to you, ladies and gentlemen. The films that we've seen, all the literature that is at your tables—the entire program that we make available to you here this evening—represents material that has been submitted to your Department of State at Albany, New York, for your protection. And certainly we're most happy that you enjoy this protection.

In a 1970 interview with the *Miami News'* Alan
Gersten, ITT Community Development president
Norman Young boasted that the aura of regulation
had been good for business. "The best thing that
happened to the land business were [sic] the state
and federal laws that keep out the fly-by-nighters.
If the customer knows he has consumer protection,
it helps us when we try to sell land."

At times, the federal government's land-sales regulators themselves have been more than willing to
boast of their promotional effect on the business they
were commissioned to regulate in the public interest.
HUD's Office of Interstate Land Sales Registration
(OILSR) had barely been in operation for 10 months
in February 1970 when it expressed its satisfaction
that "Americans are buying more lots in land subdivisions today with greater confidence under a consumer protection law. . . ."

The Office of Interstate Land Sales Registration
operates under the Interstate Land Sales Full Disclosure Act, introduced in 1966 by Senator Harrison
A. Williams, Jr., Democrat from New Jersey, then
chairman of a subcommittee of the Senate's Special
Committee on Aging. Finally enacted in 1968, the
Williams law requires any subdivider offering 50 or
more lots of less than five acres each in interstate
commerce to register with the Department of Housing and Urban Development. The subdivider is also
required to provide HUD, and each lot buyer, with
certain information about the land for sale. If the
"property report" is not given to the buyer, he may
void the contract at any time by simply notify-
ing the seller. Further, if the report is given to the

buyer less than 48 hours before he signs the contract —as is almost always the case in the high-pressure, now-or-never business of land sales—the buyer has 48 hours to reconsider his decision and rescind the contract. At present, such protection does not extend to those who buy lots during or after a personal visit to the property, or who sign a waiver.

The information required in the property report includes: a general description of the property being offered for sale, its topography and location in relation to nearby communities; any mortgages or liens on the property; the availability of utilities and their cost; recreational facilities; the number of occupied houses currently in place; drainage and/or landfill necessary for construction; availability of schools, medical facilities, shopping, and public transportation; accessibility of lots by road; and the existence of adequate markers to permit the buyer to locate his property.

There are 19 major items required in the property report, and they do indeed provide vital information for anyone contemplating the purchase of land anywhere. Yet in the purchase of subdivision lots under typical circumstances, under pressure from a salesman trained in sleight-of-mouth, the property report is next to useless. In form and content, it is a forbidding document, dealing with liens, escrow accounts, encumbrances, easements, covenants, mineral rights, and other technical matters often difficult for even the educated layman to understand. Even a land lawyer might require more than the 48 hours the law grants the unsophisticated lot buyer to study the dense language and make a rational decision.

More important is what the property report does not include. Surveys indicate that most purchasers of lots in large, remote subdivisions are persuaded to buy land for its investment value. Certainly the assurance of investment profits and ready resale are the lures used by sales people from coast to coast. Yet the property report is not required, and never volunteers, to disclose any information pertaining to the investment value of the lots being offered. Such information might include accurate data on population trends in the area, and local inventories of already-subdivided lots and underbuilt residential areas. It might also include a sales history of the land being offered, including the price the subdivider paid for it, to show how much appreciation is already included in the lot buyer's price. The current market price of comparable land near the subdivision would also be valuable. So would a resale history of lots in the subdivision, comparing the purchase price with the price received on resale. There might even be a census of lots in the subdivision currently for sale by the subdivider, or for resale by lot owners, in order to give the new investor some idea of how long he might have to wait in line before he can cash in his chips at any price.

Even in regard to the important questions it does cover, however, the property report is misleading. It affects the dignity of an official document, responding to official questions under penalty of the law. Yet, at the same time, the OILSR completely disowns the information in the report. After the disclaimer, "this report is not a recommendaton or endorsement of the offering . . .", the required notice on the front of the property report goes on: "nor has [the OILSR] made an inspection of the property nor passed upon the accuracy or adequacy of this report or any promotional or advertising materials used by the seller." In other words, the government has asked the questions, the seller has responded, and from there on out it is *caveat emptor*. Penalties for misinformation on the property report—$5,000 and one year in jail—are rarely, if ever, invoked.

One reason for infrequency of prosecutions under the law may be that the subdividers are allowed so much leeway in their responses that they can mislead without resorting to proveable falsehoods. Instead, they commonly hedge their answers to questions about the availability of water and other utilities, community facilities and the like with grand references to "plans," what the developer "believes" or "anticipates." To the unsophisticated potential buyer, such ambiguous assurances in a government-sponsored report may well seem like guarantees. In fact, however, they are not, and there is a wealth of past experience not ordinarily available to the individual buyer to suggest that the subdivider's "planned," "projected," or "anticipated" visions may never become realities, at least not unless and until the buyer pays for them himself.

The OILSR's failure to require full disclosure of all pertinent information in the property reports, or to insist on unambiguous disclosure of prevailing conditions and future commitments, and to make the whole thing clear and readable to the average layman, is not due to any lack of authority under the law. The federal statute creating the system of property reports specifies what information they must include, but it also stipulates that they "shall also contain such other information that the Secretary [of Housing and Urban Development] may by rules or regulations require as being necessary or appropriate in the public interest or for the protection of purchasers." It may well be that OILSR's lack of effectiveness in regulating the subdividers has less to do with a lack of power than with a lack of clear purpose. As an office in HUD, OILSR represents the kind of institutional conflict of interest that comprises so many Washington agencies. HUD's major concern is the encouragement and promotion of real-estate development in order to provide adequate housing for the nation. In this context, dealing with inappropriate subdivisions and land-sales promotions is distracting, if not downright counter-productive.

As originally conceived by Senator Williams, OILSR was not meant to be a part of HUD at all; rather, it was intended to function as an arm of the Securities and Exchange Commission. Under the SEC, lots in promotional subdivisions would have been regulated along with other securities. The land-sales contract would have been seen for what it really is: not the purchase of a piece of land, which has little present value and does not belong to the "buyer" until the contract is paid up, but the loan of venture capital to a developer in the hope of eventual profit when and if the subdivision comes to fruition.

Furthermore, the SEC is in the business of regulating offerings of speculative investments to the public, not promoting them. In the process of regulating conventional securities over the years, the

SEC has developed disclosure requirements that go far beyond the minimal standards of OILSR. Under SEC regulation, for instance, a company like GAC could not get away with assuring its land customers that its Poinciana subdivision is "a smart long-term investment in your future . . . whether you are able to live there or not," and permitting its sales people to suggest extravagant fantasies of future profits, at the same time that the company was telling customers for its debentures that "there is no significant resale market for installment contracts."

In 1966, when the Interstate Land Sales Full Disclosure Act was first proposed, it promised to live up to its name under the SEC's direction. SEC chairman Manuel F. Cohen testified to a Senate subcommittee that the proposed law "basically follows the pattern of the Securities Act of 1933, which is generally recognized to have dealt successfully with the problem at which it was aimed. We believe that the same technique could successfully be used in the regulation of the interstate sale of subdivision lots." Evidently, the prospect of full disclosure and vigilant surveillance was uncongenial to the industry, however, and a strenuous lobbying campaign, spearheaded by the National Association of Home Builders, succeeded in having the regulatory function moved to the otherwise-preoccupied precincts of HUD.

In its early years under HUD's aegis, OILSR did not distinguish itself for vigor in controlling interstate land-sales abuses. OILSR activities were overseen by HUD assistant secretary Eugene Gulledge, who immediately before taking on that office had been presi-

dent of the National Association of Home Builders.
The first administrator of OILSR was the same Alfred
J. Lehtonen who left government service in 1971 on
the well-known shuttle between government regulatory agencies and the industries they regulate,
landing as a vice president of Horizon Land Corp.
Under this regime, until mid-1972, the OILSR had
secured indictments against only four subdividers,
all of them small fry, and obtained one conviction.
Sales had been suspended at only 18 projects. Dissatisfied consumers testified that their complaints about
deceptive sales practices were ignored for as long as
two years, and sometimes greeted with hostility by
the HUD regulators.

In March 1972, however, HUD Secretary George
Romney brought the OILSR under his direct pur-
view and appointed a new administrator, George
K. Bernstein. Barely two months after taking office,
Bernstein announced a nationwide OILSR road-
show to 17 cities to hear complaints from consumers
about interstate land-sales practices. "We're going
throughout the country to find out what problems
they are having," Bernstein announced, "and to identify the fast-talking, silver-tongued sharpies who are
causing those problems. Equally important, we want
to let the public know there are remedies for many
of these problems and to advise them of their rights."

The OILSR tour was widely publicized in the
press, and succeeded in eliciting reams of testimony
from angry and frustrated consumers. Months after
the year-long series of hearings was concluded, the
OILSR was still receiving 250 unsolicited complaint
letters every week. In addition, Bernstein found evi-

dence of massive noncompliance with the basic requirements of the law. "The hearings showed that many, many developers have not bothered to register," he charged. "We are going to try to track them down." Despite his obvious good intentions, energy and determination, Bernstein's ambitions to regulate the industry may exceed his resources: his total staff numbers some 50 people, only 16 of whom are involved in investigative work.

In an effort to curb some of the most deceptive sales practices, Bernstein's office announced in early September 1973 that, beginning December 1, subdividers would be required to offer more information to consumers in their property reports. The new disclosures include a warning in red that "purchaser should read this document before signing anything" and a certified statement of the subdivider's financial condition. Promises of future improvements to the land must be accompanied by an "expected" completion date. Advertising for subdivision lots "must not be inconsistent with the information contained in the property report," and "shall not misrepresent the facts or create misleading impressions or inferences." The same prohibitions apply to sales people's pitches.

However, there is little in the new regulations to inhibit the sale of subdivision lots as blue-chip investments. And the strictures on advertising and sales practices may still be loose enough to allow room for nimble land hustlers to dance circles around the truth. The timetable required for all promised improvements, without severe penalties for failure to deliver or a bonded contract of completion in advance, may prove to be worth no more than a sched-

ule on the Penn Central. Still, the new regulations
are a welcome step toward reform. On paper at least,
they seem to promise the consumer hell-bent for
self-deception some protection against his own worst
instincts and the best efforts of the promoters. Only
time will tell how effective the new rules will be in
inhibiting the enthusiasm and imagination of the
land hustlers, or how enthusiastic and imaginative
the OILSR can and will be in enforcing them.

Meanwhile, in the absence of effective federal regulation, the job of consumer protection has been left
largely to the individual states. While 35 states presently have legislation requiring the registration of
subdivision offerings, uniformity ends there. Nine
states—California, Georgia, Kansas, Maine, Minnesota, Missouri, Tennessee, Vermont and West Virginia — take the position the federal government
rejected in 1968 and regulate interstate subdivision
offerings as securities. California is schizophrenic in
this regard: out-of-state subdividers must run an
obstacle course of security and real-estate regulations
in order to offer lots to Californians. The subdivider
must bond himself for the completion of promised
improvements within a limited time. Claims of investment value for the lots must be justified. Most
important of all, California carries out a detailed,
on-site appraisal of out-of-state subdivisions, in order
to determine the "fair, just and equitable" price the
subdivider will be permitted to ask. Not surprisingly,
out-of-state subdividers are scarce in California. But,
ironically, California's home-grown land hustlers,
such as the California City promoters, flourish under
much less stringent rules and enforcement, and they

have the lucrative, land-happy California market all to themselves.

California's law regulating intrastate subdivision sales, as well as similar consumer-protection laws in other states, follows the federal example in relying mainly on disclosure in the form of a property report or offering statement. Among the state laws, New York's is commonly considered one of the best. Enacted in 1936 and amended in 1963, New York's legislation is reflected in some of the language of the federal act, but at least until the recent strengthening of the federal law, New York's law went further. Its disclosure provisions include the requirement that the subdivider list his assets, liabilities and income, as well as provide descriptions of the land and improvements, utilities, recreational and other facilities, conditions of sale, encumbrances on the land, and other vital factors. Along with the offering statements of some other states, New York's is accepted by the OILSR in fulfillment of the requirements of the full-disclosure act. In addition to disclosure, the New York State law requires that all out-of-state subdividers provide access by road to all lots offered to New York residents, and that any promised improvements not in place at the time of the offering be secured by a completion bond or funds in escrow.

However, the consumer is left unprotected by the state's inability to enforce the law. The rules and regulations provided for in the law state that "at a sales meeting, reception, party or gathering . . . copies of the offering statement . . . will be publicly displayed and given to each person in attendance." At none of the dozen or more sales dinners and meetings attended during the research for this book was the offering statement in view or proffered. Quite the opposite: the statement was more often concealed and stubbornly withheld. Specific requests for it were met on various occasions with blank stares, as though the sales person had never heard of the document; protestations that the offering statement is only given out after a contract has been signed; assurances that nobody reads it, though "you should" —in a tone of voice that made it clear that it was only for the over-cautious. On one occasion, when a salesman finally handed over the offering statement, he was publicly reprimanded by the sales manager. At many New York sales sessions, the offering statement is presented only after a contract is signed, lost in a packet of colorful promotional literature. From that moment, the customer has 48 hours to decipher its tortuous language and, if he then wants to rescind the contract, to locate and inform the subdivider.

Like the OILSR, the secretary of state's office in New York can claim that it does not have the capability to enforce its own rules. According to Harold Harris, a public-relations spokesman for Secretary John P. Lomenzo, budget cutbacks have forced the department to stop policing land-sales dinners and to curtail other enforcement activities, even though "we've never had so many land offerings as we have now. . . . New York is where the market is." Abuses of the law at land-sales dinners and meetings, he said, were due merely to "over-enthusiastic salesmen —the developers can't control them." When he was told that one AMREP saleswoman had assured a customer that the secretary of state himself was the author of the Rio Rancho contract, Mr. Harris replied simply, "You wouldn't buy a piece of land just because somebody told you the secretary of state wrote the contract, would you?" A senior attorney responsible for handling subdivision complaints in the secretary of state's office excused the lack of aggressive enforcement with the observation that "we have to maintain an ongoing relationship with the developers. Besides," he asked, "how do you prove a violation of the law" at an off-the-record land-sales dinner? Evidently, he was not considering the obvious method of sending state investigators to monitor such proceedings.

According to the secretary of state himself, "Most sellers of subdivided land will agree that purchasers should be afforded every possible protection under the law." The New York State law, Secretary Lomenzo continued, results in "better consumer protection. As in all areas, fortunately, the unscrupulous are minimal. . . . In New York State we take pride in the fact . . . that our system of consumer protection in land purchase is most effective."

One indication of the effectiveness of New York's consumer protection is the fact that in 1970 the residents of New York State were offered 100,000 out-of-state lots for a total price exceeding $250 million. In that year, enforcement actions by the secretary of state's office against illegal land-sales practices resulted in refunds to abused customers of a mere $128,290. The following year, 91 out-of-state subdividers offered 150,000 lots, with a total price tag of $375 million.

19.
Save
the land,
save
the people

Even the most ambitious consumer laws may prove unable to protect people from their own blind lust for an iota of the American landscape, their own readiness to lunge for the merest shadow of a dream. At least in a technical sense, most lot sales can be considered transactions between willing sellers and willing buyers, and there are moral as well as constitutional hazards involved in trying too closely to monitor human nature on either side. There are certainly practical problems as well in any effort to prescribe the script of every encounter between sales people and customers, and to proscribe every conceivable deception by innuendo, inference, or tone of voice. The more exhaustive the legislation, the more exhausting it would be to enforce. It might be argued that beyond a certain point people ought not, may not, or cannot be protected from themselves.

Nevertheless, a total laissez-faire policy would leave both the land and local communities wide open to the mischief of the subdivision promoters. As an alternative or complement to consumer legislation, therefore, an increasing number of states are enacting innovative controls on the use of the land itself, thus limiting the subdividers' access to their basic resource. At this writing, federal legislation to assist and encourage all states to undertake land-use planning programs is halfway through Congress. Senator Henry M. Jackson's bill (S 268), passed in June 1973 and awaiting reconciliation with whatever land-use bill emerges from the House, directs the states to plan for "areas of critical environmental concern," such as wetlands and wilderness. It also prescribes attention to developments that would have a major impact on the landscape, including major subdivisions. Although the Jackson bill, with administration support, includes sanctions in the form of withholding certain federal funds from noncomplying states, its critics charge that the bill lacks explicit standards for state land-use-planning policy. While Congress deliberates, a patchwork of land-use regulation is being established by the individual states.

In Florida, for instance, where both the consumer and the land have been notoriously and woefully abused by subdividers for decades, land-use legislation has outpaced consumer-protection measures. The recently enacted Environmental Land and Water Management Act gives the state the power to identify and limit "developments of regional impact." The most important section of the act empowers the state to designate up to 5 percent of Florida's land inventory as "areas of critical state concern." Once an area is so designated, standards for its protection and appropriate development can be legislated. Then the protected land can be released from the control of the act, and the "critical concern" shelter can be moved to another threatened area.

Florida has also enacted land-use laws directly limiting subdivision activities. One, for instance, simply requires companies selling lots of less than two and one-half acres by installments to satisfy local platting requirements; in effect, this will mean that all lots must be accessible by road. Assuming that local regulations are well written, the new law will make it impossible for a developer to sell underwater land, or even lots on floodplains or in swamps where roads cannot go. Another recent law requires subdividers to get state permits for all dredging and filling operations before they can sell the lots. Had ITT, for instance, been obliged to obtain prior state approval for its canal building, Palm Coast might never have happened; nor might many of the other subdivisions created by draining Florida's ecologically priceless wetlands.

California took a significant first step toward state-wide land-use control in 1972 with the passage of the Coastal Protection Initiative, popularly known as Proposition 20, after its short title on the ballot. The passage of the citizen-sponsored legislation establishes a "coastal zone," extending generally from the ridge line of the coastal mountain range seaward to the three-mile limit. Within the coastal zone, a protected "permit zone" extends inland only 1,000 yards from the high-tide mark. Development activity within this permit zone is to be limited by regional commissions until the end of 1975, when a comprehensive plan for the protection and rational development of the entire coastal zone is to be submitted to the state legislature.

Proposition 20 was on the 1972 ballot in the first place because conservationists and their allies in the state legislature—notably Assemblyman Alan Sieroty of Beverly Hills—were unable to get their coastal-protection bills through the Senate. The cause of the difficulty was identified by John Berthelson of the *Sacramento Bee*: a quiet group called the Committee Opposed to Ecology Groups, composed of 34 industry lobbyists, including representatives of Southern California Edison, Standard Oil, and the California Real Estate Association.

Blocked in the legislature, the California Coastal Alliance, coordinating agency for dozens of California environmental organizations, went to the people. With 408,815 signatures on a petition, they got Proposition 20 on the ballot in 1972.

The election campaign was a David-and-Goliath affair. The opposition forces enlisted the political public-relations firm of Whitaker and Baxter, and funded them with a $1.1 million war chest. At least 227 corporations, including prominent subdividers, contributed to the battle against Proposition 20. The outcome was so important to developers everywhere that much of the anti-20 money came from outside the state. For their money, the bankrollers got billboards warning, "Don't let them lock up your coast. Vote No on 20" and "Conservation Yes, Confiscation

No." There were also television spots showing the beautiful California coast and urging viewers to protect it by voting against the proposition. Even Governor Reagan, an opponent of coastal legislation, had to admit publicly that the industry campaign was misleading.

On its side, the Coastal Alliance had very little money for media advertising. Instead, it drew on help from volunteers, including such celebrities as Lloyd Bridges, Charlton Heston and Doris Day. To supplement the advertising budget, Sierra Club lawyers got an FCC order granting free air time to counter Whitaker and Baxter's radio and TV blitz. "The Sierra Club supports Proposition 20 . . . Signal Oil opposes," said one of the ads. "You can tell a proposition by the company it keeps." On November 7, the voters of California endorsed Proposition 20 by a 55-to-45 percent margin.

No sooner had the proposition carried, however, than the opposition began to sabotage it by securing the appointment of pro-development allies to the district commissions. Not a few coastal developers simply disregarded the commissions' power of approval and went ahead with their projects, either because a delay would cost too much money, or because they refused to recognize the new status quo.

Nevertheless, it is evident that the protection afforded approximately 8,000 square miles of California's coast is hurting developers. Three landowners quickly filed a class action against state and regional officials in the name of all property owners, claiming that they were the victims of "confiscation" of their private property rights without just compensation. Their suit asks for $509 billion—half a trillion dollars, or almost $100,000 per acre.

Some existing coastal subdivisions, as well as those projected for the future, find themselves constrained. Sea Ranch, the elegant project on the rocky coast of Sonoma County, now attaches a special note to its offering statement warning that "AFTER FEBRU-ARY 1, 1973, PERMITS WILL HAVE TO BE OB-TAINED FROM A REGIONAL COMMISSION FOR ANY DEVELOPMENT WORK WITHIN THE PERMIT AREA.... PROSPECTIVE PUR-CHASERS SHOULD INVESTIGATE AND CON-SIDER HOW THE INTEREST THAT THEY WILL ACQUIRE IN THIS SUBDIVISION WILL BE AFFECTED BY THE REQUIREMENTS OF THE NEW LAW."

In its readiness to experiment with new-fangled notions, Vermont is more than a mere continent re-moved from California. Vermont's orthodox theology of private-property rights and local control is as stub-born as the rocks in its cow pastures, making the state unlikely ground for the growth of land-use legisla-tion. But in recent years, Vermont's traditional in-sulation in the northeast corner of the country has been ended by the interstate highway system, bring-ing affluent refugees from the cities of Massachusetts, Connecticut and New York. Aside from clean air and unspoiled scenery, Vermont's main attraction is win-ter sports, especially skiing. The slopes that make Vermont dairy cows grow short legs on the uphill side also afford the best skiing in the East, and people with the money for a pair of slats and poles and all the other paraphernalia required to ski and *après*-ski also have the money to buy a piece of Vermont for their very own and put a house on it.

But the slopes that are so good for skiing, and even better for scenery, are ill suited to the kind of intensive living that subdividers have been all too quick to impose on them. The soil on Vermont's hillsides tends to be shallow, a few feet deep in some places, a few inches in others. Unlike the Southwest, Vermont's problem is not less water than it needs but, in some places, more than it can readily absorb. The 30 to 40 inches of annual rainfall tend to run downhill rapidly, either on the surface or down the face of the underlying bedrock. The loss of ground cover, soil disturbance, and paving and roofing that go along with subdivision developments create ideal conditions for erosion and flooding.

Moreover, the shallow soil has only a limited capacity to absorb or filter sewage. Most subdividers, however, prefer to spare themselves the front-end cost of adequate sewage-treatment facilities, so each housebuilder is forced to install his own septic system. The wastes that mix with the groundwater pollute downhill wells. In the cold skiing weather, the septic system's bacterial action is slowed, and untreated wastes come to the surface to add a certain sweet savor to the fresh Vermont air.

Many subdividers have simply overwhelmed local governments accustomed to administering small-town affairs and huge, unpopulated acreage. Much of the Vermont landscape is conveniently held in vast, readily divisible tracts by timber companies. For companies such as Vermont Lumber and International Paper there are obvious advantages in exchanging the modest but perpetual annual profit from sustained-yield forestry for the instant bonanza of subdivision profits, just by drawing lines on a map and hustling the little squares to outsiders. For their part, the land-rich, tax-poor towns are convinced that subdivisions will end their financial woes, or they are simply blitzed into acquiescence.

In 1972, however, Vermont began to fight back. By then, the state's population was growing at a rate of 1.8 percent a year, and two-thirds of that was immigration. Fully 30 percent of the state's land was owned by out-of-state residents—both corporations and individuals—according to Governor Thomas P. Salmon. The 40-year-old Democrat was elected that year by the orthodox Republican state on a platform including a strong land-use-control plank. Salmon's first step was a law formally identified as Title 10, Chapter 151, Vermont Statutes Annotated, but popularly known as Act 250. In the face of the inability of the Vermont towns to cope, the act reasserts the zoning and planning powers that the states have traditionally abdicated to local jurisdictions.

Act 250 requires the state to adopt the basic tool of land-use planners: a land-capability survey measuring the inherent capacity of the land to sustain development. This is to be the basis for a plan suggesting appropriate future uses for various categories of land. To secure conformity with the plan, Act 250 sets up a system of approvals for any new development or expansion of existing development involving more than 10 acres, or more than one acre in towns lacking zoning and subdivision regulations. The would-be developer must satisfy a district commission on 10 specific counts. He must demonstrate adequate safeguards for the quality of the air, water and soil, and for the effect of his plans on local community facilities such as roads, schools and hospitals. Existing local land-use plans must be respected. And, in an extraordinary advance, the act requires that the proposed development "will not have an undue adverse effect on the scenic or natural beauty of the area, esthetics, historic sites or rare or irreplaceable natural areas." A companion law, Act 252, establishes standards for water quality strict enough to move one local observer to comment that "you can't spit in a Vermont stream."

Vermont developers were still assessing their losses from Acts 250 and 252 when Governor Salmon and his allies came up with another legislative weapon against land exploitation. In April 1973, the state moved to skim the cream off the exorbitant profits from land speculation. With the price of desirable land rising 20 to 25 percent a year in some areas, huge profits were being made by speculators who simply held raw acreage for a short time and then resold it. The new law imposes a graduated capital-gains tax on such easy profits. The tax is based on the length of time the land is held and the rate of profit on the resale. Thus, a speculator who doubles his money in less than a year will pay 45 percent of his gains to the state; or 60 percent, the maximum, if he does twice as well. At the other extreme, if he holds his land for five years and makes less than a 100 percent profit, his capital-gains tax is only 5 percent. The excess-profits tax does not apply if the land is held for more than six years.

According to Governor Salmon, the tax's inhibiting effect on land speculation will "give us additional running room, to give local communities a greater opportunity to evaluate the disastrous consequences of bad planning." The opportunity is unwelcome to many Vermonters. While much of the dissent may be motivated by obvious self-interest, it is often based on substantial legal or constitutional arguments. "I question further curtailments of the right of people to own and use land," says state Senator Fred Westphall. "What we're doing is destroying the concept of the private ownership of property. I don't believe you can justify this under the federal or state constitution." Another Vermonter, a lawyer, calls the game by name: "In effect, this is a taking of the property legislatively rather than through the eminent domain process." In any case, Senator Westphall dismisses the possibility of damage to the state by subdividers. "We've been selling swamps and mountains to 'smart' people since Ethan Allen's day," he says, "then buying them back and selling them again."

Vermont's new legislation is destined to be bitterly contested in the courts, along with the plan for Adirondack State Park in New York, California's coastal legislation, and similar laws enacted by other states looking for a mechanism to check abuses by subdividers and other developers. The notion that the government, acting for the people, has the power to limit development rights on private property has never been taken for granted in America. The more common assumption is that traditional private property rights confer on the landlord the absolute discretion to develop the land any way he chooses. In this view, development rights inhere in the land as a function of ownership, and any limitation of those rights is subject to the constitutional prohibition against taking private property without just compensation. Those who favor land-use controls claim that development rights belong to the public, and can be limited by government for public purposes without penalty.

The issue is so basic to American philosophy, and the practical effects of the outcome so momentous, that the validity of land-use control must ultimately be decided by the Supreme Court in the context of emergent public opinion. But at least until the issue is decided, land-use laws offer the most effective defense against the multiple mischief of subdivision hustlers, who take advantage of private property rights to abuse both the land and the public. While the public can defend itself against the subdividers, if only it will, the land cannot. And, as is so often the case where the interests of people and land intersect, if we take action to protect the land we cannot help but protect ourselves.

PAGE 69: *The Stars and Stripes'* descriptions of sales techniques are in its 1972 series, *op. cit.*

PAGE 71: Merrill Jensen's observations on Benjamin Franklin's land-promotion activities are taken from his essay "The Articles of Confederation," *op. cit.*; and his article "The Creation of the National Domain, 1781-1784" in *The Mississippi Valley Historical Review,* Vol. XXVI, No. 3, Dec. 1939, Copyright © 1939, Mississippi Valley Historical Association.

PAGE 85 *ff:* A full discussion of water-resource problems in New Mexico and the Southwest is contained in the report "Where Has All The Water Gone?," prepared by the Central Clearing House, 338 East de Vargas Street, Santa Fe, N.M.

PAGE 87: The quotation is from *Damming the West:* Ralph Nader's Study Group Report on the Bureau of Reclamation, by Richard L. Berkman and W. Kip Viscusi. Grossman Publishers, New York, 1973.

PAGE 100 *ff:* The fate of subdivision legislation in the New Mexico legislature is chronicled in *The New Mexico Review,* March 1972; *El Independente of Santa Fe County,* May 26, 1972; and a report compiled by 13 students at the University of New Mexico for a class in legislation. The student report, as well as helpful correspondence, were provided by Norman L. Gagne, one of its authors.

PAGE 107: State Senator A. T. Montoya was killed in an automobile accident on January 14, 1973. His brother, Theodore "Ted" Montoya, was named to fill his unexpired term.

PAGE 110 *ff: The New Mexico Review* reported thoroughly on the pueblo subdivisions in its issues of October and November 1970, and November 1971. John Soper published a series of articles on Cochiti Lake and Great Western United in *The New Mexican,* August 24-29, 1971. Other reports on the subject appeared in *The New Yorker,* December 18, 1971, by Calvin Trillin; and *Harper's Magazine,* January 1973, by Eric Treisman.

PAGE 133 *ff:* Much of the documentary material on California land use and abuse is included in *Power and Land in California,* a 1200-page report by a Ralph Nader study group under the direction of Robert C. Fellmeth and assisted by funds from the Sierra Club Foundation and the Abelard Foundation. A condensed version of the full study is published under the title *Politics of Land* by Grossman Publishers, New York. The alacrity with which the findings of the study were disowned and defamed in California testifies to both its accuracy and the paranoia of some Californians in response to criticism from the press.

PAGE 136: The history of Shelter Cove is reported fully in an essay, "Buy A Little Bit of California For Your Own" by Lou Cannon, published in the Winter 1967/68 issue of *Cry California; The Journal of California Tomorrow*, 681 Market St., San Francisco.

PAGE 140: The source of the quotation from Harold Berliner is his essay "Plague on the Land" in the Summer 1970 issue of *Cry California*, published by California Tomorrow, of which he is a founding father and officer.

PAGE 142: A detailed expose of the California City operation is in *Politics of Land, op. cit.*

PAGE 148 *ff:* Much of the chapter on Boise Cascade is drawn from the investigations of Harold Berliner, *op. cit.* and elsewhere; and Lynn Ludlow, published in the *San Francisco Examiner*. Another valuable source is *Politics of Land, op. cit.*

PAGE 178 *ff:* All quotations from Barry Lessinger are from a telephone interview with the author.

PAGE 184 *ff:* Professor David's remarks were made at the New Communities Conference held by the American Institute of Architects in Washington, D.C., November 3-6, 1971.

PAGE 188: Quotation from Harold Berliner, "Plague on the Land," *op. cit.*

PAGE 195 *ff:* The California Senate testimony is taken from the transcript of joint hearings held by the Senate Local Government Committee and the Senate Select Committee on Urban Affairs in Sacramento, December 7 and 8, 1970.

PAGE 199: Quotation from Harold Berliner, "Plague on the Land," *op. cit.*

PAGE 200: Figures on the costs vs. benefits of development are quoted from *Equilibrium*, Vol. 1, No. 1, January 1973, published by Zero Population Growth, Palo Alto, California.

PAGE 201 *ff:* Quotations from Irv Hensch and William McMillan are taken from telephone interviews with the author.

PAGE 217 *ff:* The Cumberland Island story was reported in *The Atlanta Journal,* December 21, 1972; and *The Atlanta Constitution,* December 22, 1972.

PAGE 221 *ff:* The establishment of Point Reyes National Seashore was chronicled by Lynn Ludlow in the *San Francisco Examiner,* August 18, 19 and 22 and September 19, 1971.

PAGE 224 *ff:* David Bird and Myron A. Farber of *The New York Times* covered the battles over Adirondack State Park during 1972 and 1973.

PAGE 238 *ff:* GAC's long and tortuous history as a subdivider is detailed in *The Great Land Hustle,* by Morton C. Paulson, published by Henry Regnery, Chicago, 1972.

PAGE 258 *ff:* Morton Paulson's book, *ibid.,* also contains an interesting account of the establishment of the OILSR.

PAGE 268: Harold Harris made his remarks in a telephone interview with the author.

Index